"Sarah Bereza has written a book I wish I had when I was starting out in ordained ministry! She helps anyone who is in professional, public ministry consider the issues related to being authentic to oneself while being responsible to one's role. This is a must-read for every new pastor!"
—Bishop Karen Oliveto, Mountain Sky Conference,
The United Methodist Church

"Being fully ourselves in public ministry is a challenge for religious leaders. Authenticity can feel elusive. Sarah Bereza offers not rules but a lens for navigating this terrain with theological and ethical grounding. She frees us from believing that we must act the same way in every situation to be truly ourselves."
—Lovett H. Weems Jr., Distinguished Professor Emeritus
of Church Leadership, Wesley Theological Seminary

"In this honest and helpful book, Sarah Bereza traces forms and seasons of ministry that can ring hollow. A minister can feel or appear hypocritical when the role they play by virtue of the office they hold bumps against a not-infrequent dissonance with their own struggles, doubts, or evolving theologies. Listening with a careful ear to her own experience and probing through interviews of the experiences of dozens of practicing pastors, teachers, and musicians, Bereza is a welcome companion to any on the journey of professional ministry, ordained or lay."
—David M. Greenhaw, President Emeritus,
Eden Theological Seminary

"This is a must-read for professional leaders of faith communities who strive for integrity between their public role and perception and their personal identity and desire to be fully themselves."
—Bishop Kenneth L. Carder, Ruth W. and A. Morris
Williams Distinguished Professor Emeritus of the Practice
of Christian Ministry, Duke Divinity School

"In this important and approachable book, Sarah Bereza provides a series of helpful lenses through which Christian leaders in public ministry can understand themselves in relationship to the individuals and communities they serve. With characteristic wit and keen insight, Bereza moves the discussion beyond popular buzzwords like *authenticity* and *sincerity*, providing new models for navigating pressures and struggles as a 'professional Christian.' A must-read for ministers and those preparing for ministry."

—Monique M. Ingalls, Associate Professor of Music,
Baylor University

"Sarah Bereza is a highly gifted interviewer and writer. This book is a treasury of wisdom for any who follow the call to Christian leadership."

—Jeremy Begbie, Thomas A. Langford Distinguished
Research Professor of Theology, Duke University

"'I would be true, for there are those who trust me,' goes the hymn by Howard A. Walter, a call that challenges all who are in vocational Christian service. In view of this, Bereza offers wise counsel on how leaders can be their genuine selves in their ministry."

—Lim Swee Hong, Director of the Master of Sacred
Music program, Emmanuel College of Victoria
University, University of Toronto, Canada

PROFESSIONAL CHRISTIAN

PROFESSIONAL CHRISTIAN

*Being Fully Yourself
in the Spotlight of Public Ministry*

SARAH BEREZA

WESTMINSTER
JOHN KNOX PRESS
LOUISVILLE • KENTUCKY

First Edition
Published by Westminster John Knox Press
Louisville, Kentucky

22 23 24 25 26 27 28 29 30 31—10 9 8 7 6 5 4 3 2 1

Unless otherwise indicated, Scripture quotations are from the New Revised Standard Version of the Bible, copyright © 1989 by the Division of Christian Education of the National Council of the Churches of Christ in the U.S.A., and are used by permission.

Book design by Drew Stevens
Cover design by Nita Ybarra

Library of Congress Cataloging-in-Publication Data is on file at the Library of Congress, Washington, DC.

ISBN-13: 978-0-664-26671-4

Most Westminster John Knox Press books are available at special quantity discounts when purchased in bulk by corporations, organizations, and special-interest groups. For more information, please e-mail SpecialSales@wjkbooks.com.

For Crawford Wiley

CONTENTS

INTRODUCTION

So deeply do we care for you that we are determined to
share with you not only the gospel of God but also our
own selves, because you have become very dear to us.
—1 Thessalonians 2:8

Public ministry trains a spotlight on us, illuminating some
aspects of who we are, while casting other features into
shadow. The small slice of ourselves that people see in the
spotlight reveals real and true things about us, but we are
far bigger than we appear in any instance—like a sermon, a
conversation, or a photo—in which someone else encounters us. Even the people we've known and loved for years
cannot know us as we know ourselves and as God knows us.

While many people in public-facing jobs encounter
a similar gap between the fullness of who they are and the
slice that others see in public settings, those of us in ministry often encounter more barriers to being fully ourselves.
Whether we are on staff at a church or work in a religious
organization like a school or nonprofit, we have serious
responsibilities as leaders in our communities: We represent faith and even God to many people. We are often held
to higher moral standards than people working in similar,
but nonreligious, fields of employment. We have certain
kinds of power over the people we minister to and with,
and we're often put on a pedestal as role models.

As professional Christians, our employment—the
means by which we pay for our daily bread—intertwines

with our personal faith and with the beliefs and expectations that congregants, denominational leaders, or other organizational authorities have for us. In the United States, our employers have virtually limitless latitude in hiring and firing on religious grounds, and in many instances, the people we lead also wield financial power over us. While some of us made a knowing commitment to certain moral standards during our ordination process, what may have been unclear is that something as ordinary as clinical depression could lead to our employment being terminated. Even the waxing and waning of faith—so common, yet so rarely talked about—could bring financial uncertainty.

For many of us, being fully ourselves also means that we must negotiate between our gut feelings and ministry settings that specifically prevent those emotions from immediately surfacing. Whether we're caring for people through illness, counseling them through dark seasons of their lives, or simply leading Sunday services through the ups and downs of our own lives, we have a job to do, and to do it well, our spontaneous feelings often take a backseat to the needs of the people we serve.

Despite the difficulties, we must strive to be fully ourselves because it is good to be who we are. God made each of us unique, precious, complicated, and bigger than anything that paper and ink, or screen and pixels, can capture. All the bigness, all the beauty God made is good. In the broad contours of who we are and in our specific characteristics, God has given us our own ways to be in the world and to live into our spiritual gifts, including through our occupations in ministry.

We can disagree whether or not a cosmic fall has fundamentally marred our goodness, whether "all our righteousnesses are as filthy rags" (Isa. 64:6 KJV) means that something is wrong in our core, or whether an "ancestral curse" or "original sin" has a place in our self-understanding. Whatever our different views, we Christians agree that we are each made in God's image, that we bear God's imprint, and that a major goal of our life is continually conforming to the image of Christ. In that regard we are fundamentally good, no matter what we think about the rest.

Because we can better minister with God's gifts to us when we are more ourselves, thriving in ministry does not have to come at the expense of who we are. As we conform more to Christ, others see more of Christ in us. When our neighbors do the same, we see more of Christ in them. Christians have realized for centuries that being close to God doesn't mean that our own selves fade like fabric in the light of God's presence. Rather, to paraphrase a modern example, "when we are wholly God's, we will be more ourselves than ever."[1] The closer we are to the blaze of God's glorious light, the more our truest colors shine.

A ROADMAP TO BEING OURSELVES IN MINISTRY

In this book, we'll first explore the foundation for *being ourselves*—shorthand for *being fully ourselves in the spotlight of public ministry*. Then we'll examine seven obstacles we often face as professional Christians. The first is that many people see us as faith representatives that they trust and hold up as role models, or perhaps immediately dislike and believe to be hypocrites. Whether or not we want the responsibility, we may find it difficult to be ourselves given the additional weight our words carry with some listeners.

Second, we don't have an excellent conceptual framework to talk about what being ourselves can mean. Concepts like authenticity and sincerity, though helpful, are also flawed.

Third, much as we want to love our neighbors, we sometimes struggle to identify who they are and experience a blurring of lines around whom we are responsible for in ministry. We used to have a good sense of who our neighbors were and could be: anyone we encountered. However, in the age of the unlimited, often anonymous, internet, our neighborhood can feel as if it has gone from a finite number of people to an unmanageable sea.

Fourth, because of the spotlight on us, we must actively decide what parts of our lives to make public. Even when we realize the importance of protecting our privacy and energy, the act of curating what others see of us in public may feel like a fundamentally dishonest practice, as if we are pointing our cameras at a pretty vase of flowers while a mountain of dirty laundry looms outside the frame.

Fifth, being in the spotlight also means that we navigate the valid (and not so valid) ways that others' needs impact what we share publicly. For instance, whether we are preachers facing Jesus' words on divorce in a lectionary cycle of Scriptures or teachers coping with national politics in our classrooms, we must decide how and when to tackle hard issues.

Sixth, we all live through valleys and seasons of transition, but we cannot always share them publicly out of respect for professional boundaries, personal privacy, and the privacy of others. Maybe we are waiting for the results of a medical diagnosis or caring for a loved one through their mental illness. Maybe the denominational home that used to fit like a glove feels not only uncomfortable but wrong. It is difficult to discern how to live through these seasons with integrity.

Finally, we must often be fully focused on other people in the midst of their own joys and concerns, no matter our own feelings. We may be personally joyful but ministering to someone on their literal deathbed. Or we may be uninspired when it is our responsibility to lead corporate worship. Holding our personal circumstances and emotions to the side, even temporarily, can feel disingenuous. All these obstacles, yet our heartfelt desires remain to be truly ourselves, to be seen as we truly are (How wonderful the moments when we can say, "I feel seen"!), and to minister to our neighbors from the complex depths of our souls.

This book explores these difficult areas in both the broad strokes and the details of our lives, sometimes to find solutions, sometimes to get at an unresolvable tension, but never simply to apply a Band-Aid or encourage a self-destructive way out. We've seen those fake solutions and maybe tried them for ourselves: the emotional detachment that doesn't transform the fundamental facts of our lives; treating ministry as purely social work, a reframing that removes "Christian" as an integral aspect of our profession but still doesn't remedy the problem; scrunching into an ill-fitting job; finding temporary escape through alcohol or other drugs.

So instead of superficial hacks or a list of dos and don'ts, this book gives you a lens. This lens will help you understand how your full self relates to the incomplete picture that other people have of you in public ministry. And it will help you develop the tools you need to engage with the challenges and opportunities stemming from this reality.

A MULTITUDE OF COUNSELORS

Our own life stories and circumstances significantly shape our perspectives, giving us "situated knowledges."[2] This is why, drawing on my doctoral training in ethnography, I interviewed fifty other professional Christians as I wrote this book (though I use the term "professional Christian" to account for the wide range of occupations and roles in full-time ministry, not everyone I interviewed identifies with it). By bringing their voices to the question of how to be fully ourselves, we gain the wisdom of a multitude of counselors—their situated knowledges of public-facing ministry based on their varying personalities, ages, and so on. For more information about these interviewees, see the list in the back of this book.

Their knowledges include perspectives gleaned from many aspects of their lives, including their ministry roles (such as pastors, youth leaders, and teachers) and their experiences as ordained and nonordained people (approximately 65 percent of the former and 35 percent of the latter). They are Roman Catholics, Evangelicals, Eastern Orthodox, Oriental Orthodox, Pentecostals, historically Black Protestants, and mainline Protestants. Their theological leanings range from conservative to progressive. I interviewed approximately the same number of women and men, encompassing a range of sexual orientations and identities. They include abled and disabled people. All live in Anglophone countries (Australia, Canada, England, and the United States). They include Asian, Black, Hispanic, Middle Eastern, and White people. Finally, for many I interviewed, their knowledge comes from ministry beyond their local settings through media like writing and speaking. While none of them is perfect—of course they aren't!—they are all people to whom I reached out because I thought, "They seem to navigate the ministry spotlight in a healthy and professional way. I should learn from them."

MY STAKES IN BEING FULLY MYSELF

My situated knowledges include a broad perspective on denominations. For over twenty years, I have ministered on staff and as a volunteer leader in a wide variety of denominations from Evangelical to mainline Protestant and Roman Catholic; I grew up in Baptist churches and became Eastern Orthodox as a young adult; and I have attended services at dozens of Evangelical churches as an ethnographer. Since I began ministering as a musician at a young age, my primary experience of churches has been as part of a leadership team, not as a solo staff person or as a layperson in the pews. These experiences, mostly in denominations that I am not personally affiliated with, have been a source of joy as I have encountered the many ways God leads us corporately.

My situated knowledges also include being a White person in a biracial (Hispanic and White) family of origin and interracial (Asian and White) marriage with biracial children. My knowledge comes from being in my mid-thirties and being sometimes student-poor but mostly middle-class. I wrote a large portion of this book during the COVID-19 pandemic, which caused a host of disruptions and constraints, and underscored the oddities of being myself in an online season of ministry. (Who knew I'd ever lead a church book study in pajamas or chop veggies during coffee hour, much less nurse a baby in staff meetings?)

Finally, my situated knowledges come from a longstanding sense of being particularly challenged in my efforts to be myself.[3] This feeling is partially due to my personality, yet much of my ongoing interest in being myself, not just for my personal fulfillment but in the broader questions this book addresses, comes from my experiences as a child and adolescent in independent, fundamental Baptist churches with leaders who self-identified as fundamentalists. While I intended to leave this circle of Christianity since I was a tween, I spent over a decade untangling myself, a journey that rarely afforded me the space to be anything but a slim approximation of myself, and that often led to my feeling like I was lying by existing as well as I could.

As you can imagine, my formation in fundamentalism greatly shaped my perspective on the relationship between our own selves and how others perceive us in the spotlight of ministry. First, my experience of fundamentalism was of a profound responsibility to *appear* godly. Yes, also to *be* godly, but with a strong emphasis on how others perceived me and my behavior. For instance, my family watched some movies but didn't watch them in movie theaters because, even if we were watching an approved film, someone might wonder whether we were watching a bad one if they saw us at the theater. In this book, I take a very different angle on others' perceptions: we can't determine these (mis)perceptions and shouldn't give them too much weight, though we are foolish to ignore them entirely.

Second, beginning in middle school—around the same time that I realized I would eventually leave fundamentalism—I became the pianist (the main musician) in my church. As I grew increasingly alienated from the theology and resultant culture in the church, I continued to lead musical worship there for years. I was aware of this disintegration at the time, but until I wrote this book, I didn't understand that the issue was not only a personal one (in that I didn't fit there), but also a problem of leadership.

Third, growing up as I did in the nineties and aughts, my broader evangelical zeitgeist was one of a self-proclaimed "authentic faith." To me, it seemed like a lame attempt to make Jesus cool and relevant in a knock-off "if you like this sexy music, here's some Christian Lite to try" kind of way. I've been allergic to the word "authenticity" ever since and have steered clear of commodities purporting to make me more authentic if I cough up the money. (Admittedly, I do occasionally purchase things I hope will make me cooler, to no apparent effect.) Though in chapter 3 I explore how authenticity is a concept that gives us insight into how to be fully ourselves, I remain suspicious of Christian branding attempts to make faith cool, a.k.a. authentic.

Taken together, these formative experiences sparked my research into how vocalists communicate their personal beliefs while leading worship (an aspect of my academic research focusing on theologies of music, worship, and liturgy; fundamentalist Christianity in the United States; and racism in musical discourse and performance practice) and continue to motivate my personal and professional interest in the question of how we can be fully ourselves in public contexts, particularly ministry-related ones.

LOVING OUR NEIGHBORS AS OURSELVES

As we approach the question of how to be fully ourselves in public ministry, I want to ground us in the most crucial thing of all: love. Much of this book is directly or indirectly about loving our neighbors. "Neighbor" can mean anyone, but here, I use "neighbor" to mean someone we interact with. A neighbor can be someone listening to our recorded sermon, someone reading what we've written, or someone in the pew on Sunday morning singing alongside us. Calling these people "neighbors" (rather than "congregation" or "audience") rightly reminds us that even when we are communicating and don't hear our neighbor's response, we're still in a kind of relationship with them.

Loving our neighbors as our whole selves is not an easy road, but it is the one that God continually calls us to walk. Pastor Paul Rock points us to the truth: "The way the Gospel is going to be most effectively communicated is through you being brave enough to be yourself and allow the Spirit of God to speak through you and your beautiful imperfection." We can't let fear lead us to create a false persona that others can criticize in lieu of our true selves. Instead, we must embrace the truth that counters this fear: only as our individual selves can we conform to the image of Christ and, in so doing, love God and love our neighbors.

KEY TAKEAWAYS

As we grow into the image of Christ, we become more and more fully ourselves. It is only as our individual selves that we love God and love our neighbors.

Being a professional Christian means that our livelihoods are contingent on our personal faith. This brings a host of complications to being fully ourselves in the spotlight of public ministry.

Our life stories and circumstances shape our perspectives, which is why this book includes a wide range of interviewee voices in addition to the author's.

DISCUSSION QUESTIONS

1. What are times that you have experienced being more fully yourself as a way to love God and your neighbors?

2. What consequences have you experienced from having your faith tied to your livelihood? Do you think of yourself as a "professional Christian"?
3. What kinds of situated knowledge do you bring to your ministry?

Chapter 1

THE FOUNDATION FOR BEING
FULLY OURSELVES

We may believe in the importance of being ourselves in ministry, but in the slog of daily life—when we're tired, overextended, and don't want to kick up controversy—living into that fullness can feel impossible and irrelevant. How much easier to stay small, stay in our lane, check off our daily to-dos, and save our whole selves for another day. Yet when we don't share ourselves in that God-made fullness, we are hiding our God-made light under a bushel basket. When we hide that light by consciously putting ourselves into settings that conceal it, we're not only harming ourselves; we are obstructing God's gifts to us and our neighbors.

You may agree with my premise that God made each of us good but question the wisdom of focusing on the pursuit of our fullest selves, because it could encourage our tendencies toward self-centeredness or be an exercise in navel-gazing that keeps us from leaning into whatever work God has called us to. This is the sentiment Cynthia G. Linder describes in her research on pastoral ministry and personal complexity, which she calls "multiplicity." She finds that calling attention to multiplicity can feel selfish or peripheral to ministry. Maybe you have had an experience similar to that of the pastors she interviewed: "The practitioners themselves had often not recognized this ministerial multiplicity as resource or resilience, nor had this multiple-mindedness been sought, affirmed, or cultivated by the institutions that played significant roles in their ministerial formation."[1]

This multifacetedness—an integral aspect of being ourselves—enriches ministry, as Linder shows throughout her work. While her research focuses on ordained pastors, it seems likely that the same would also be true for other ministry leaders. The people I interviewed, both ordained and nonordained, experienced a similar strengthening of their ministries as they became more fully themselves. Summing up the relationship between personal complexity and pastoral ministry, Linder writes that the "pastors who ministered effectively in complicated settings were people who were themselves complex. They exhibited multiple interests and gifts, inhabited multiple roles, experienced themselves differently in multiple settings—and it was precisely this ability to move between roles and worlds nimbly and creatively that afforded insights and occasions for innovative pastoral practice."[2] When God calls us to ministry, God calls the many facets of ourselves that inform how we follow that call, in all our personalities' strengths and weaknesses, our interests and passions, and our personal histories.

To follow that call with all of our hearts, we must have self-knowledge and a willingness to grow as ourselves in Christ, develop close relationships where we can be truly vulnerable, and work in an environment that allows us room to be ourselves. The importance of these factors may seem obvious, but many of us know colleagues who lack self-awareness or whose personal growth seems to have ended in adolescence. We've seen what happens when people don't have solid close relationships: unhappiness, oversharing, and inappropriate friendships. We've met people whose jobs hemmed them in instead of nourishing them. For the most part, these colleagues didn't end up in those situations because they were dumb or naive, but because of how difficult it is to lay a strong foundation for being ourselves. Even though we can spot the deficiencies in other people, we ourselves can easily end up in the same place. Maybe we rightly understand that our identity isn't in our job, but do not realize how much the particulars of a job affect our ability to be ourselves. Maybe the question of how to be ourselves has been in the background—"the white noise of my life," as pastor Jorge Acevedo describes it—as our actions flow intuitively from our values and personalities until we land in a setting where we must actively evaluate how to be ourselves. Maybe we begin professional ministry and then discover we can't be vulnerable with as many people as we could before. Perhaps we just need a job (any job!) and then learn that, while it's great to be able to pay the bills, being a square peg in a round hole is exhausting and leads to burnout. So we must be intentional in laying our personal and professional foundation.

SELF-KNOWLEDGE AND GROWTH

A child will naturally grow to their full potential height, unless stunted by specific genetic or environmental factors, but personal growth and maturity don't happen automatically, especially not where public ministry is concerned. We develop our whole selves only when we are intentionally motivated by a belief in the value of self-knowledge. "Communicating yourself as a genuine person requires a lot of interior work," notes homiletics professor Kenyatta Gilbert. He's not alone in making this observation. The majority of people I interviewed mentioned the importance of tools like therapy and spiritual direction for intentionally gaining the self-knowledge we need to be ourselves. They also pointed to a rich engagement with their pasts to inform how they understand who they are today—what writer Rozella Haydée White describes as "going back to my creation story and making sense of it, not only as an individual but in my family and culture."

This interior work entails a clear-eyed perspective on our flaws and a willingness to let go of those flaws, even if we think of them as part of our core identity. Being made in the image of God "doesn't mean we're going to be sinless" but, rather, "that we're made in this image of greatness," explains theology professor Lakisha Lockhart, "so we shouldn't be afraid of greatness. We shouldn't be afraid of the good we can do in the world."

Yet sometimes we are afraid of that greatness, partially because of people who label their self-centered, obnoxious behavior as "just who I am." Those people may not think they are perfect, but they seem to believe that being themselves necessitates hanging on to their worst characteristics and most selfish tendencies. You may have heard someone say, "Well, he thought I was rude, but I was just telling it like it is." Or perhaps, "This is just who I am; so, she had better get over it or get out." Often it is adolescents who confuse being themselves with weaponizing themselves, while adults fearfully swerve into the opposite lane with politeness and bland peacekeeping that they mistake for loving their neighbors.

If becoming our most whole selves means conforming more and more to the image of Christ, then being ourselves can never mean being a jerk or a doormat. As we come to terms with ourselves, we have to learn what our weaknesses are and grapple with our worst tendencies. In humility, we must open up ourselves to growth in Christ and the goodness we can bring into the world.

This growth is ongoing. It's not as if we can figure out who we are and maintain that identity for the rest of our lives. Back in grade school literature class, I learned that some fictional characters are considered dynamic, and some are considered static. The dynamic characters change in the course of the narrative, while static characters remain the same. But in real life, we are all dynamic.

On the surface it might not seem intuitive that we change throughout our lives. Most of us can look back on the last decade of our lives and realize we've changed, but we may mistakenly think that *now* we are fully formed and won't change much in the future. Researchers have termed this the "end of history illusion."[3] In the findings of Jordi Quoidbach, Daniel T. Gilbert, and Timothy D. Wilson, "young people, middle-aged people, and older people all believed they had changed a lot in the past but would change relatively little in the future" in the areas of their personalities, values, and preferences.[4] The research team found that, contrary to what people believed about their future selves, the study participants *did* change over time, regardless of their age.

Part of being ourselves is that lifetime of transformation. As homiletics professor Eunjoo Mary Kim succinctly put it, "Being authentic means every moment to be changed. Being authentic doesn't mean just sticking to who I am now, because my Self is open to the future." If we want to follow the Holy Spirit's leading into the future—and I hope we all do—we can't close our minds and hearts or harden our attitudes and assumptions. We must be willing to grow, change, and be transformed.

That said, this book is not about that kind of interior work, but about communicating our genuine, evolving selves in the context of professional ministry. It's not about discovering who we really are, personality frameworks, letting go of the shame that limits many of us, unearthing and examining the family systems that have shaped us into our current selves, or any of the other tools that help us increase our awareness of who we are and who we can be as we grow in Christ's image. This book assumes that we have already done that interior work to some extent and made an ongoing commitment to growth in Christ. We will discuss here the question of how we interface with our neighbors through our ministry relationships and public self-presentation.

Personality

When I began writing, I consciously solicited interviews from people in a wide range of denominations, ages, ethnicities, and so on. I couldn't predetermine personality types—though it takes a certain kind of personality to say yes to an interview that delves into your experience of being yourself, especially if you don't already know the interviewer personally. For some people I interviewed, being themselves came easily; if it didn't, there was an external factor (like a wrong job) that, once corrected, eliminated the problem. Put this kind of fish into the right pond, and they swim with ease, without self-consciousness, seemingly without a learning curve. Many others told me one reason they said yes to my interview request was that they had had the experience of *not* always feeling true to themselves in public spaces. They had grown in this area, sometimes struggled in this area, or seen other people's difficulties and tried to learn from them.

Depending on your past experiences, you may assume that the people with personality traits like being more extroverted or gregarious were the people who found that being themselves came more easily. However, that's not what I found as I interviewed. None of the differences in a person's willingness to be themselves seemed related to personality features like introversion or extroversion or being more or less gregarious. Some of the people I talked with who appeared to be the most extroverted had relatively little to say about themselves in the sense of articulating what being themselves meant to them personally. The crest of energy many extroverts find in some aspects of public ministry, and the corresponding exhaustion it yields in some introverts, didn't seem to cause or even correlate with their respective abilities or willingness to be fully themselves in those settings. Instead, the key factors were whether the individual had a foundation in their life that allowed them the room to be themselves and had an ongoing discernment of how to be themselves in the various situations and circumstances of their lives.

VULNERABLE RELATIONSHIPS

Let's move to the second aspect of our foundation: relationships. You probably already realize how critical close relationships are—relationships where you can be completely vulnerable, relationships that hold your most complex and messy experiences, that care for your rawest emotions. The difficulty isn't in realizing you need these relationships at all, but in recognizing how important they become when you are in professional ministry, and how, for those of us working in churches, particularly as pastors, those close relationships can no longer be with the congregants we serve, because of the power differential between us. If you were raised in the church, you may be used to your closest relationships growing out of the fabric of the congregation. Even though we can still be vulnerable and bring difficult experiences into that ministry space, our most vulnerable relationships are now outside of our congregation instead of within it.

Moving to the professional side of ministry can also make us more aware that Christian people are just people, with all the messiness that being human entails. Unless we grew up with deep ministry connections (such as having a parent who is a pastor) and have already grasped this fact, we may grow disappointed and burdened by the emotional weight of the pastoral care many of us give.

As a result, we need relationships of vulnerability coupled with counsel (whether formally, as with a therapist or spiritual director, or more informally with trusted colleagues), to make sense of this challenging aspect of ministry. Leah D. Schade, an ordained minister and seminary professor, tells me, "I have a place to go with whatever the residual is from this emotional roller coaster. And it's not in a bottle of alcohol, and it's not in a bottle of pills; it's in a person that I can confide in and who I trust to help me work through this." People rely on our counsel, and we need people who can be that counsel for us. "It's their job to do for you," Schade continues, "what you do for everybody else—listen, help you process, and offer guidance."

This shift in how we relate to people who aren't in professional ministry isn't a form of deception, and it isn't a way of making ourselves smaller. "It's just being human and appropriately so," explains musician Robert McCormick. By embracing the relational fullness that is part of being human, we emulate Jesus, our model of perfect humanity—Jesus, the one who went away from the crowds to be with his closest friends, who wept with Mary and Martha. Thinking of those stories, pastor Magrey deVega says, "I'm imagining Jesus in those self-contained, safe contexts with those disciples, just letting out another side of himself because he was fully human." McCormick and deVega, like many others I interviewed, point to how they need these closer relationships to be in the fullness of themselves.

Close Relationships and Criticism

One important aspect of our close relationships is how those people can give credible criticism and critique of us and what we do. Criticism is always with us, and our fear of it—for many of us, more prominent than the fear of failure—can color much of our public-facing work. *What kind of backlash could this sermon provoke? Will people think I'm dumb if I . . .?* It takes bravery to show up and minister, knowing that simply doing our jobs, and doing them as ourselves, will provoke criticism that is truly of us, not a facade we're hiding behind.

We may also experience others' criticism of our public work as criticism for who we are. Easy as it is to conflate *who we are* with *what we've created* (or even *what we do*), we may get caught up in that lie and attach our self-worth to whatever we've created, then become disillusioned if others don't receive our work positively; or we may try to avoid their criticisms by taming our work to fit what we imagine others want. Although being ourselves involves creation, the things we make aren't us. What we make isn't where our worth lies and never will be. So, when the criticisms of our work come—and they almost surely will—we must hear that criticism for what it is: a criticism of what we've *made*, not of our self-worth.

The problem isn't that criticism is never helpful, but that not everyone is a legitimate source of criticism in our lives. We must consider their legitimacy as a commentator and put their perspective into context with our other relationships. Often others' criticism is about them, not us and our actions, and this reality is heightened for professional Christians, where the biting criticism we receive may stem from how others see our roles as faith leaders or from their beliefs about God. Pastor Philip DeVaul points out that "when someone is in charge and has a position of authority or responsibility, our gut reaction is to assume that they're strong enough to take whatever we've got"—with criticism to match.

Our close friends and counselors, on the other hand, see us as ourselves, not just through the lens of our roles or an aspect of our public work. They are the ones who get a legitimate voice of criticism in our lives. It takes a lot of courage to rain on your friend's parade and a lot of humility to be able to hear critique, especially if our friend or mentor isn't always a clear communicator (and who of us is all the time?). We may hear their criticism and disagree, but we can trust in their good intent and care for us.

Pitfalls and Warning Signs

Leaning into our closest relationships is not always intuitive when we first begin professional ministry. But if we don't shift, we will likely veer into oversharing or isolation, or even find that we are more able to be ourselves around strangers than with our friends.

Oversharing, where we bring more private parts of our lives into settings where intimacy is not warranted, is the more obvious pitfall. We've likely all experienced sermons that made us cringe, met pastors who treated congregants as their buddies, or known bosses or teachers who wanted to be our best friends. It's not enough to hear the classic warning that "the congregation is not your therapist" and nod our heads. We have to actively protect ourselves from this type of oversharing through active discernment. What may be appropriate for a congregation where we've ministered for decades—a congregation that's seen our kids grow up and met our grandkids—is different from what is appropriate where we've barely made it through a program year together. We may share something in a Bible study that we wouldn't in a sermon, even though that information might be shared through the grapevine, because the power relationships in one-to-one conversations differ so markedly from the megaphone of a sermon, as does their spiritual mandate.

Isolation is a less obvious pitfall but no less challenging. Here's how pastor Amy Miller confronted the isolation that was her initial experience in ministry. At first, she tells me, she felt as if she couldn't be vulnerable anywhere— "like there was no space for me, like nobody really wanted to know all of me, nobody really wanted a chance to love all of me." As Miller grew as a pastor, she began to understand how different relationships have different depths with corresponding levels of vulnerability. Now, she visualizes relationships as a series of concentric circles, with the closest relationships at the center. In her ministry, the outer circle is the congregation in general. Next is the larger worship team she leads, which begins to deepen relationships. Then comes the smaller worship team. On this team, she has an increasing level of vulnerability. "These are the people that I would cry more with," but, she says, "the focus is more on them in their journey than me in my journey." The next smaller circle is her staff colleagues, where she can focus more on herself. And then at the center, where she can be most vulnerable, are her closest friends.

Finally, our interactions with relative strangers can be a warning signal that something is amiss with our closer relationships. Being ourselves around relative strangers can sometimes be more straightforward than it is with closer friends. With strangers, we may more easily imagine personal growth and change. We may also find that we can share difficult circumstances more readily with them because we don't expect deep care and concern in these casual encounters, whereas we do expect that response from the people closest to us. Relative strangers aren't as invested in our futures and what becomes of us. They aren't familiar with our histories, even in the banal details like what color our hair was a few years ago, so they aren't as likely to respond in surprise when we change or tell us that our actions are unlike us. "Strangers, unconnected to our pasts and, in most cases, to our futures, are easier to experiment around," writes Priya Parker. "With strangers, there is a temporary reordering of a balancing act that each of us is constantly attempting: between our past selves and our future selves, between who we have been and who we are becoming."[5]

This difference isn't necessarily a problem but can point to one. "When we fail to be ourselves in human relationships," comments writer Nicole Roccas, "what we are really saying to those that love us is that we don't trust them. We don't trust them to see and accept us for who we are, in all our strengths and weaknesses."[6] If we repeatedly feel the need to act differently around strangers or to seek out relative anonymity, it can be because our closest relationships are constraining rather than nourishing our fullness.

FINDING A NOURISHING WORK ENVIRONMENT

Our work environments are the third aspect of our foundation because our jobs determine how we use most of our time in support of our beliefs and values. Whether we are ordained in a denomination that determines our local job placement, or able to minister across a spectrum of nonprofit organizations, most of the important factors of our work environment are fixed before we arrive, from their denominational histories and their codes of conduct to their spoken and unspoken values and cultural norms. This makes our workplace a vital factor in how we can be ourselves. "Get it right," says nonprofit leader Kim Smolik, "and you don't have to make the choice each day" to be yourself, because you've already made it. But get it wrong, and you have no hope of being yourself, no matter how much you try.

It may seem like the most obvious thing in the world that we should try to work in environments that align with our core values, but often we don't. When we begin ministry, many of us don't understand how critical our work environment is, especially if we aren't ordained, because we haven't realized how uniquely privileged the religious elements of our jobs are. Clergy usually have years of discernment and training before they are ordained, a process that includes consideration of denominational specifics and how personal beliefs and values align with them. But for most lay religious jobs, formal training typically doesn't have these kinds of conversations, since most of these professions have primarily nonreligious employment options.

For instance, a science teacher working in a religious school probably wouldn't have a complete understanding of what their choice entails, since their training wasn't geared toward that setting. A musician could accept a position at a Presbyterian church without realizing where it lies along the spectrum of conservative to progressive Presbyterian denominations. They could begin working in a Roman Catholic parish, without appreciating how many factors depend on the current priest and bishop, and how much could change with subsequent ones.

Even when we try to be fully aware of our choices, the inner workings of our environment can be convoluted, even contradictory, in ways that are not immediately apparent. We're encouraged to speak up on hot-button issues—until a significant donor disagrees with our viewpoint. We're supposed to be a voice of youth—but only if that voice accords with the boilerplate on the church's website. Our organization's code of conduct doesn't match how our congregants live (or how they believe Christians in general should live)—but we must follow it. We're hired as a token to show up and look good in photos—not to help lead any real change.

The constituents of our faith-based organizations—whether they are parents and students, congregants, or board members—often hold a wide range of views with a relatively small number in common. Additionally, those constituents' viewpoints may be not only different from each other but in opposition to each other. Indeed, some of their views may be opposed to an organization's stated values. For instance, a congregant may be willing to be in a congregation with different values than their own, as long as those values are not too prominent and as long as the congregation's leaders do not speak up too much about them (that is, they "aren't divisive"). This dynamic leads to a gulf that leaders must navigate between different groups of congregants; this often results in leaders "being deeply circumscribed by people who are concerned about fundraising," as pastor Jude Harmon aptly puts it.

Despite that plethora of viewpoints among the people we serve, as employees of the organization we may be expected to limit ourselves to the small area where everyone agrees. "I feel like the church wants to have it both ways," explains Sandhya Jha, an ordained nonprofit leader. "It wants to present that we're all equal, and then it wants to withhold the ability to be one's full self from the pastor."

Musician Dan Forrest gets at the heart of the issue as he describes the criticism he receives for engaging in civic and political topics on social media. Even though people camouflage their complaints in the language of faith—"You have a great platform for music and Christianity, but don't spoil all that by talking about politics; you should just talk about the Bible and about music"—their issue is with the fullness of self that he brings to his work. Forrest explains, "Just because I'm a musician doesn't mean I'm not allowed to have opinions or that I can't possibly share anything of worth on any other front. There's so much horrible repression of personhood there. . . . You want me to provide the products or services that you like, but you won't let me be a complete person."

People making this kind of criticism will always be with us. What matters is how we personally respond and how our workplaces support us when people try to keep us in that narrow overlap of all the constituents' views.

What We Can Do to Find a Good Work Environment

One excellent way of discerning whether our workplace encourages us to live out our core values is through our ability to speak up about contentious issues and to speak from our values about those issues. Paul Vasile, a musician and nonprofit leader, tells me, "I have been able to speak up, and I have been able to say more than I thought I might, with the confidence that I'm with people who are also sharing those values." He's able to do this because he's in a workplace that not only allows his values but nourishes them.

However, speaking up on something close to our hearts isn't necessarily literally linguistic; it is also a metaphor for the bigger picture of our professional work. Smolik tells me, "I don't think being authentic means you have to speak your mind on everything all the time. I don't think I'm being inauthentic if I don't get a chance to wade in on those conversations or viewpoints. I do think I'm being inauthentic if I am not doing work where I feel most aligned with my deepest values." Because her deepest values are aligned with the mission of her workplace, the choice to be herself "is already in place."

Since what is controversial varies widely, we have to carefully gauge our own priorities and evaluate potential employers accordingly. Most of us can't engage on every topic all the time, but we often know what issues are close to our hearts (you can probably identify a couple of issues off the top of your head). With those issues in mind, we can determine what values and beliefs we need to be living publicly and consider how our workplace encourages or discourages them. There are sometimes legitimate reasons to stay in an environment where we have to stifle our impulse to speak up. But if we quiet our voices long-term, we risk silencing them entirely in our efforts to remain integrated within ourselves.

Another way to discern a workplace's support for us as whole people is to be as transparent as possible from the beginning of a hiring process, and then never let up. We may not be able to uncover all of a potential employer's implicit values and policies, so the onus is on us to be ourselves from the get-go. "People should know about who you are, and what you think and believe about things," explains pastor Brandan Robertson. "Sure, it might cost you some positions, but in the long run, it is so liberating to know that my congregation knows who I am."

Finally, though we need to be aware of the immovable aspects of a new job, we also need to remember that we often can influence our work environment, sometimes greatly, depending on our position and power. "We get to shape the culture" where we minister, points out pastor Jorge Acevedo. Among the many factors that we can shift, many church and nonprofit leaders told me about intentionally pushing their work cultures toward what Acevedo terms "appropriate vulnerability," especially as they model it in their own lives. Robertson, for instance, connects his actions with a change in his church's culture, where people seem to be "able to lean into their authentic selves a little bit more." He explains, "As I've gone down this path of trying to be radically authentic and drawing strong boundaries about who has authority to make judgments about my life, it's not only helped me live what I think is a freer, more authentic existence, but I've seen it work towards the benefit of other people as well."

Giftedness and Growth in the Workplace

Even settings that don't actively stifle us may not draw out our best qualities, leading to a feeling that pastor Molly Baskette describes as "dancing together, but we keep stepping on each other's toes." The clumsiness isn't ill intentioned, but it can lead to second-guessing that is far from nourishing. Better to be in relationships and jobs where we are encouraged to shine and where we can also help bring out the best in our colleagues.

We can be most fully ourselves when our jobs help us grow in our strengths and allow us to spend most of our time in those areas. It may seem selfish to focus on making sure *my* job fulfills *me*, but this kind of self-focus makes us able to minister fully. "Working out of our gifts is not exhausting, and it doesn't make us feel resentful: it fills us with a lot of fulfillment and energy," explains pastor Lydia Sohn. "When I am feeling really fake or exhausted or resentful, it's a sign to me to figure out, am I doing something that doesn't really give me life?" Working from our strengths can be the most demanding work we do, but it is also life-giving, both to ourselves and to those we serve.

The importance of working out of our strengths is one reason many professional Christians embrace a range of roles or skills. That variety within a single job allows us to use a broader range of our strengths. Schade says, "There are so many facets to my own personality that if I were only in one setting, I would never get to explore them." She notes that "it's all the real me," throughout a ministry that includes preaching, scholarship, and activism.

Yet our many and varying strengths can also lead to our feeling conflicted when considering different jobs, even though it's simply an outgrowth of our being multifaceted people who consider jobs that draw on different aspects of who we are. For instance, I have felt that my tailored resumes reflected poorly on me because I could truthfully say, "I want *this* job," and justify it with one set of qualifications, while simultaneously saying, "I want *that very different* job," and justify it with another set of qualifications. One of my friends, after proofreading a set of my applications, laughed and said, "It's amazing how different you seem in these letters, but it's all completely true."

Our workplaces won't exercise every strength that we have or fulfill every value, but they can bring out something special in us, something that God has particularly given. "I oftentimes say, if you place a microphone before me, something happens within me, like I click on. . . . I come alive in a way that is not disingenuous," says writer and speaker Cara Meredith. We all have areas where our work brings out something profound about our calling. Maybe, for us, as for Meredith, it's public speaking. Perhaps it's teaching or being with people who are dying. These gifts don't disappear when we are tired. They cannot be erased, even if we feel fragmented or think we're not fully showing up as ourselves. Whatever the gifts are, our workplace needs to exercise them. When our work environments call us to be more fully in these specific gifts, we are more and more fully ourselves as God has made us to be.

"Regardless of how bad my week has gone and regardless of how bad that morning is going, when I step into that pulpit, for the next twenty minutes, everything feels right, from the moment I first start preaching until I do that closing prayer." That's how deVega describes how significant his experience of preaching is in the context of his whole life. He says it is the "most consistent reminder of the genuineness of my call to ministry," because of how the tension of living life, with its ups and downs, is "transformed" in that time. He observes, "There is a different sort of existential being that I have where it all fits together—everything that I am and everything that I'm doing. Even if it's all chaotic everywhere else, it just feels right. That has always happened. And so I have to say: That is grace. That is absolutely not me."

God gives us all gifts, and if our work environment is to nourish us, it must have room for us to use them, and people who encourage us to do so. We might think we know what it means to be fully ourselves, but what we can imagine alone is often smaller than what we can dream up in community with others. "The power of our Christian community is that we not only expect more of each other," says pastor Brian Erickson, "but we also see potential in each other that maybe we wouldn't otherwise see." This potential isn't just in the facets of ourselves that are most present in public ministry. It can "permeate the areas your congregation doesn't see."

Finding this potential also depends on our relationships in the workplace, not just the on-paper aspects of our professional environment. We might work with outstanding people who don't truly get us or encourage us to grow; maybe individual relationships make sense, but the collective energy drains us. On the other hand, we can work with people who build us up in ways we haven't even imagined.

Because of the power of our community, the baseline for being ourselves is a workplace where we can use our skills and exercise our values, and relationships where we can be appropriately vulnerable. The question shouldn't be whether these relationships or environment inhibit us, but whether they encourage us to grow into our strengths. Do the people closest to us and the people in our workplace help us grow more and more ourselves as we follow Christ? Hopefully the answer is a resounding yes.

KEY TAKEAWAYS

Laying a strong personal and professional foundation is vital to *being ourselves*—and can be surprisingly challenging to do. We grow as our whole selves only through intentional development motivated by the belief in the value of self-knowledge. Contrary to what we might assume, we change throughout our lives in significant ways.

Being multidimensional enriches ministry, and differences in personality like introversion or sociability don't seem related to our willingness to be ourselves.

Our closest relationships are where we need to be vulnerable and seek out constructive criticism. If we don't make this intentional, we risk oversharing in ministry contexts or becoming isolated.

To find a nourishing work environment, we must consider how our values and strengths fit with a given position and show up fully ourselves from the beginning of a hiring process.

DISCUSSION QUESTIONS

1. What are times when you've struggled or succeeded at being fully yourself in public ministry? Is this something you have considered before?
2. Were you surprised at the research around the "end of history illusion"? How have you changed in the

last decade? How might you change in the next decade?

3. How have your relationships shifted since you entered ministry?

4. What is a time you were able to be more yourself around a stranger than a friend?

5. Can you think of something you could have shared in a previous work setting that would be oversharing in your current job or vice versa?

6. For nonordained people, what conversations do you wish you had had before getting a religiously affiliated job?

7. What strengths do you want to use in your workplace? How could you use them more than you currently do?

8. How does your job, including the people you minister with and to, encourage you to grow? How can you encourage the people around you to grow?

Chapter 2

POWER, PEDESTALS, AND OTHER COMPLICATIONS OF PROFESSIONAL MINISTRY

We want to be fully ourselves in ministry? Check. We're doing our best to be in nourishing relationships and environments? Check. With this foundation in place—one that we would hope for everyone, regardless of whether they are in ministry roles—we can turn to the next big question: What is it about being a professional Christian in the spotlight of public ministry that makes it so difficult to be ourselves?

It is already hard enough to be fully ourselves in the nitty-gritty circumstances of life (what the heck does "being ourselves" even mean on Tuesday evening in a PTA meeting?), but a host of complications arise specifically from our being professional Christians. First, people often perceive professional Christians as representatives of God or Christianity. Second, many of us have relational power, such as the power to influence others. Third, because of these factors, we are often held to high moral standards as role models in our communities. Finally, many professional Christians, particularly clergy, are both *in* religious roles in terms of their jobs and *are* those roles in terms of their identity (I use "role" rather than "office" to account for a wide range of vocations and denominational perspectives).

All four of these areas directly relate, not only to being fully ourselves in public ministry, but also to how others perceive us in our ministry roles and what their expectations are for those roles. These perceptions—and sometimes misperceptions—often have little to do with us as individuals and more to do with how our roles have been shaped by denominational histories and theological perspectives over the centuries. These factors lead some people to assume we are more morally upright and closer to God than they are; and they believe that we are worth supporting financially, as demonstrated by their donations to the organizations we work for or their purchase of materials and services we provide. The biases and prejudices like racism, sexism, and ageism that people carry with them in other contexts also affect their perceptions of us.

Regardless of how people see us through their own lenses, we know all too well that we are basically the same as everyone else. Even though others may see us as more special or spiritual than they are, we aren't fundamentally different in our humanity from our neighbors. "Everyone in ministry is on the same journey as everyone that they minister to, and that journey is becoming human," points out writer Nicole Roccas. "So we're not going to have struggles that are all that much different than the people we minister to. The more we recognize that—both as people in ministry and as people to be ministered to—the wider we make that path, and the easier it is to travel it together." We may be committed to higher standards than many of our neighbors, and our mistakes and sins can have more significant professional repercussions than theirs, but our path to God is the same.

The task is then responding to and intentionally shaping these (mis)perceptions without being puffed up or living into false expectations of who we are and what we represent.

PROFESSIONAL CHRISTIANS
AS FAITH REPRESENTATIVES

As professional Christians, almost all of us are perceived as representatives of our faith. For some people, we represent a local church, a denomination, or the church as a whole. To some ears, we sound like the voice of God. To some eyes, we are what is right or wrong with the world. Beyond these perceptions, many of us truly *are* representatives of faith, in that we have a calling to explicitly Christian activities like Bible study and leading corporate worship. "Anyone can visit people in the hospital," observes pastor Philip DeVaul, "but when you do it as a priest or pastor, it has a different connotation. The church is then visiting in that sense." Some of us are not only representatives on a local level but speak as denominational representatives. For instance, professor Tanya Riches says she feels she must comment on some global and national events because "to not say anything while all the other denominations' theology lecturers say something leaves the Pentecostals I represent in a situation that may misrepresent them."

This reality can be jarring for many of us, especially if our training didn't prepare us for it, as is the case with many nonordained professional Christians. "I'm not just speaking as a private person of faith," explains musician Robert McCormick. "Even though I willingly identify as Christian and do so with joy, I would love not to have everything I say be measured by my being a representative of the parish where I serve, because it feels very daunting."

In most congregations and some parachurch settings, we meet people who struggle to see us as individuals because of their attachment to what they think we're representing, whose past experiences have led them to have specific expectations for ministry leaders, and who criticize us if they believe we don't measure up to those expectations. For instance, if your ordination is in a tradition that understands clergy to be fundamentally distinct from other Christians, then most congregants will see you from that angle, whatever your own desires or intent. Think of how someone may have had a childhood pastor with one kind of personality, and then struggle to imagine a caring pastor who isn't a carbon copy. Even though we don't have to change ourselves to fit those perceptions, we need to know they exist.

PROFESSIONAL CHRISTIANS HAVE POWER

The power we hold in our religious spheres affects our ability to be ourselves, as does our power coming from the deference given to ministry leaders like clergy in many non-religious settings. We have to grapple with this power as we learn how to be fully ourselves in our roles, neither falling into the trap of pretending that we don't have this power (a lie that lets us off the hook in terms of our leadership), nor swinging to the other side and abusing this power, such as by setting ourselves up as unquestionable spiritual authorities.

Of the kinds of power we may have, the most relevant to being ourselves are the power we gain from knowing private information, our power to be heard, and our power to influence others. Whether we learn private information indirectly or from the people concerned, simply knowing some kinds of information gives us power over other people, since in most ministry settings they don't know similarly private things about us. This knowledge forces us to confront issues of honesty, discretion, and diplomacy. We may learn information about someone without their knowledge, or we may have information we cannot share publicly. How then should we engage in conversation around that topic without lying directly or by omission? Pastoral counseling adds additional complexity, because we usually give this care to people who know us and our families, whereas traditional therapists and their clients have a clearer social separation.

Our ability to be heard is another kind of power. I mean this in a literal sense, in that we often speak without the likelihood of people interrupting us or leaving. This power is most pronounced in sermons and other elements of corporate worship, but also crops up in other settings where we hold the floor (and the microphone). In addition to the obvious theological responsibilities we have, this dynamic is one main reason we must take care with what we say. It's also why an overly personal sermon illustration so disturbs listeners. The problem isn't just the oversharing, but that the oversharing occurs not in a conversation that others could redirect or exit, but at a time when social norms glue congregants to their seats.

Related to our ability to be heard is its metaphorical meaning: our power to influence others. In her public work, pastor Bethany McKinney Fox shares aspects of what is unfolding in the unconventional church she pastors, as a way to expand others' ideas of what's possible. "Sometimes you need to see people that are doing different things to get your own gears turning," she notes. "Sometimes you just don't know what can be done until you see somebody else doing it."

Beyond sharing ideas, the credibility we have on specific issues due to our training, roles, and on-the-ground experience means that many people will listen to what we say, even if they hold different views. One way of thinking about our relative abilities to influence is through the lens of privilege. Because of various privileges, some of us can speak up in ways that others, without those privileges, cannot. More to the point, some of us can speak up *and have people pay attention* who wouldn't listen to others with less privilege or different kinds of privilege. If we "are privileged enough to be in a position where we have the ability to speak truth to power," says pastor and diocesan leader Jonathan Arnold, then we have a corresponding responsibility to speak up. Similarly, McCormick points to his privilege when talking about the questions he gets about why he doesn't just make innocuous posts related to his profession as a musician, instead of following his conscience by fostering conversation around divisive political issues. "Sure, that would be more pleasant," he observes. "But I feel like it comes from a place of privilege, the privilege of only sharing meatloaf recipes and puppy pictures."

Church leaders, especially ordained ones, have a unique kind of influence born from many factors, including their caregiving, counseling, and the trust placed in them and their role—influence that may open ears that otherwise would tune out what they don't want to hear. Pastor, professor, and retired bishop Will Willimon explains how he sees the pastoral obligation that arises from this influence: "To me, part of the courage of saying controversial or unpleasant things is: I'm your pastor. I want to be your friend. I want to be in ministry with you, but I'm ordained, and I'm attached to the Word of God." A pastor is responsible for presenting a church's doctrine while also inviting a congregant into relationship and dialog, saying, for example: "I understand that you are having trouble with the fact that this is the historic witness of the Church. But it's my duty to tell you, 'This is the historic witness of the Church.' Can we still grow together? Can we still be in conversation?"

The Risks of Influence

Our power to influence comes with many risks as we exercise it. As a result, we need to use our influence with care. While we may think of the positive ways to use our influence, Phoebe Farag Mikhail sees the need for moderation. Farag Mikhail, a writer whose husband is a priest in the Coptic Orthodox Church, explains, "As a clergy wife, I have more influence, and as such, I shouldn't overuse it. If I'm going to influence, I want to influence you to grow in your life with God." Because of her approach, she goes deep in selected areas instead of trying to influence in all the ways she can. For instance, she writes against racism as part of her broader work on community building but doesn't address political areas that are less clearly related to faith.

When people see us in highly esteemed roles or see us leading corporate worship, we risk manipulating them. Homiletics professor Kenyatta Gilbert warns, "The more effective a person is in the persuasive act of preaching, the more that person has to be careful that they're not manipulating the people because of their gifts." If we don't take care, we may see only the positives of influence and walk right into this pitfall.

Another risk is offering opinions we have no standing to give. Because we have credibility in some areas, people may ask us for advice in other areas, even ones that we know little to nothing about. As tempting as it may be to offer our opinions, we need to be aware of overstepping our bounds. In his essay *On Bullshit*, philosopher Harry G. Frankfurt highlights this risk for people like us who are "frequently impelled—whether by their own propensities or by the demands of others—to speak extensively about matters of which they are to some degree ignorant."[1] His warning is one we all should hear: "The lack of any significant connection between a person's opinions and his apprehension of reality will be even more severe, needless to say, for someone who believes it his responsibility, as a conscientious moral agent, to evaluate events and conditions in all parts of the world."[2] Shooting the breeze with friends is one thing, but speaking in our role gives us greater responsibility to weigh our words. Although the issue is complicated by people who unduly try to insist that we don't have the right to speak up on certain topics (the classic example is being told to "stay in your lane," if you even hint at a political opinion), we must distinguish between spouting off and rightly using our spiritual background to give informed interpretations of our world.

Finally, in purposefully trying to influence others, we risk prioritizing our own perspectives to the point that we begin to believe that we are always right or the only ones who are right. We, as much as anyone else, can be self-deceived or just plain confused. (I realize by arguing that multiple perspectives can be valid, I risk appearing to believe that a crackpot conspiracy should be given the same weight as a logic-informed stance, but I'm not talking about that kind of false equivalence.) Yes, we are often experts in our field, and yes, we often have credible viewpoints—but not always, and not to the exclusion of other views.

Every one of us is "individually precious" to God, so "if you're going to be a minister to the diverse people of God, then you must keep your heart and mind open to that diversity," Arnold points out. Our histories give us one legitimate way of seeing things, but not the only one. Our situated knowledges are not the only knowledges. And, with God's wisdom our foolishness, we should never be overconfident that we have the whole world figured out. Kim Smolik, a nonprofit leader, explains, "You need everyone else around you to get the biggest possible picture of our faith and who God is." Another person with a different perspective, she continues, "is not my enemy but my teacher. They are not holding me back, but providing a broader, more three-dimensional perspective." Just as other people can see more of God in us as we conform to the image of Christ, we can see more of God in others by keeping ourselves curious about why they believe and behave as they do—an openhearted mind-set that comes only with the humility of not always being the only one who is right.

ROLE MODELS AND HIGH STANDARDS

Imagine you find out that your family physician, a professed Christian, golfs on Sunday mornings and rarely attends church services except when it rains. You might hope for an increased commitment to their faith community, but you probably wouldn't think less of them as a medical professional. Imagine you find out that your accountant, also a professed Christian, is not married but lives with their romantic partner. You might hope for them to get married, but you probably wouldn't think less of their ability to prepare your taxes.

That's not how it works for professional Christians. For us, being ourselves means adhering to specific standards that often exceed those of our nonreligious counterparts and sometimes exceed those for our fellow Christians, such as when we commit to celibacy or to following a denominational leader's directives in where we live and work. Regardless of the specific standards for professional

Christians, the key difference is the professional repercussions if we stray from them. The physician can skip church, and the accountant can live with whomever they want, but we can't. More importantly, we must live up to those standards, even if sometimes falling and getting up again, for the sake of our relationships with God and our neighbors.

As a result of these high moral standards, as well as our being perceived as faith representatives, our neighbors often see us as deeply spiritual role models, giving us an opportunity to influence people for good, but also setting us up for pride and hiding the parts of ourselves that are far from perfect. Our ability to be role models comes up throughout this book; what I want to do here is think about what we are role models of as professional Christians and how to avoid the pitfall of pride that can come from being put on a pedestal by our communities.

The risks of inflating our egos and masking our failures come down to how we relate to others' expectations. You know who you are, but other people, for whatever their reasons, think of you more highly. "They're doing that more out of the sense of their own wounds than trying to project something onto me," says John Gribowich of how he sees his interactions with people who hold him in excessively high regard as a Roman Catholic priest. "People like to gravitate towards someone or something that's going to give them the thing that they're lacking"—in this case, a balm for their own brokenness—so "whatever type of honor or privilege I'm getting from someone is more speaking of their wounds than throwing some type of demand on me." Instead of letting the deference puff up his ego, Gribowich comes back to the core relationship that we are all in as Christians: "I'm always first a disciple. And I am a disciple in the same way that everyone in the congregation is a disciple. We're all probably in different places with our discipleship, but nevertheless, we are still seeking, and we are still desiring, and we're still following. My discipleship to Jesus Christ is far more fundamental than being a pastor or anything else that I have."

Following Jesus and showing what that discipleship looks like in our faith and values are exactly what we can do as a role model: live out the goal of growing more and more into the image of Christ. Far from being a call toward fake perfection, being a role model in our communities can open us and our neighbors to God's grace. "There's a fine line between being a good role model and trying to live out this ideal of a perfect human being," pastor Quardricos Driskell tells me. "As I teach my mentees, and as my mentors taught me: I'm also still human. I will make mistakes. I will do things wrong. I will not get it right all the time. I won't get it right most times. And this is where grace and mercy come in, and I learn from those mistakes. That's a good role model! It's not being this perfect human being."

Think about it from the perspective of our commitment to high standards. Even though, in a professional sense, the repercussions for not following those standards are more severe than for other Christians, the standards are mostly the same. Remembering this fundamental sameness can allow for greater transparency in who we are. Speaking from a Presbyterian viewpoint, pastor Bruce Reyes-Chow explains, "We have different roles, but we don't necessarily have to be better people," a perspective that "comes out of a deep belief in the priesthood of all believers, that there isn't this separation" between church leaders and laypeople.

We can be role models of failure, forgiveness, grace—all in a way that will be impossible if we allow ourselves to be deceived (and to deceive others) into thinking of ourselves as exceptionally holy. When we are role models with the mind-set Driskell and Reyes-Chow describe, we aren't reveling in our egos but pointing to the Gospel as it appears in our lives. Just as a righteous person falls seven times and gets up again (Prov. 24:16), we can be role models growing in Christ's righteousness. I am not advocating for sharing our failings in a way that manipulates the people we serve, but, with forethought, we can and should make falling and getting up again part of what we visibly do as role models, as chapter 7 explores more fully.

OUR ROLES ARE PART OF WHO WE ARE

Depending on what we believe about transparency and vulnerability, acting with integrity in our roles can feel like an unbearable tension with who we "really" are, because being in a role sometimes requires that we show up when we don't feel like it. It requires that we "weep with those who weep," even if we are personally happy, and that we "rejoice with those who rejoice" (Rom. 12:15), while living through a challenging private circumstance.

Here's how Willimon describes this tension in the context of pastoral care: "I say, 'Oh, that is a terrible problem you've got, I'm so sorry.' But the truth of it may be, your problem seems terrible to you because it's yours, but it's a problem I've heard from two hundred people in my twenty years of ministry. So when I say, 'Oh, I'm so concerned about your problem,' I'm not *deeply* concerned. It's not turning me upside down. Rather, I am expressing concern because that's my role: I'm a pastor. I'm letting you know that your pastor cares about you, and your pastor is being attentive to you."

You may read Willimon's statement and think it is disingenuous. But even though our approach to this situation—a common one for those of us who lead worship or give pastoral care—has the potential both to be deceptive and to fragment us, at heart, our various ministry roles are part of who we are. They are not a layer on top of our "true" identities but are integral to our whole selves. As a result, we are being fully ourselves when we lean into a role, whether or not we feel like it in the moment.

Think of it in terms of our calling or vocation: we—our specific selves—are called to these roles. "If you say to someone, 'I'm really deeply caring about what you're talking about,' in one sense, you're not deeply caring and fully involved." Willimon continues, "In fact that would be impossible, considering all the people that you come in contact with as a pastor. But in another sense, you are, with integrity, acting out of your role." Even if we are tired, even if we don't feel like showing up, we are still being ourselves when we act in accordance with our calling, values, and ministry roles. Most importantly, we are conforming more and more to the image of Christ.

This personal identification with our role is the case even more so for clergy, as ordination in many Christian traditions is a sacrament that makes a qualitative difference in who a person is. "You're not the same person you were before," says Willimon, speaking from a United Methodist theological perspective, so your role is inseparable from who you are. "Who is the self I want to be when I'm just being myself?" he asks rhetorically, since there is no other self that isn't ordained. Even externals can be a truth about who you are, he explains: "When I put on a robe as a pastor, it's more than just a piece of clothing. It's more than an external: that robe is an expression of who I am down deep."

Similarly, those of us who are called to ministry, but not to ordination (or who are clergy in traditions that don't consider ordination to be a sacrament), are doing something in ministry that is true about us *down deep*. In the moment that we minister, we are living into the fullness of what it means for us to be part of the body of Christ as our specific, individual selves.

Leaning into a role is a part of being integrated in ministry, and we are not disingenuous if we heighten one significant facet of who we are (that is, our ministry roles) while other aspects of ourselves recede for the moment. That's fundamentally why we can show up in a role, feeling as if it's distanced from or opposed to our present emotional state, yet still be showing up fully as ourselves.

Later chapters return with this topic as it relates to ministering while we are in the middle of difficult circumstances (chapter 7), leading corporate worship (chapter 8), and giving pastoral care (chapter 8).

OTHERS' EXPECTATIONS FOR AND PERCEPTIONS OF US AND OUR ROLES

We all live with others' expectations and perceptions of us. While these external factors may spur us toward growth and a closer walk with God, we may make ourselves smaller because of them. We may get unduly attached to others' grand ideas about who we should be, even if those ideas don't match our own desires or capacities, and end up striving for our parents' dreams or blindly following our congregations' wishes.

Others' expectations may also emerge from harmful stereotypes, narrow archetypes, and misguided assumptions.

Some of us don't fit our archetypes and find that ill fit a blessing. (Shockingly, I ditch the stereotype of organists as snobby curmudgeons for my actual self without a second thought.) But many of these external expectations have troubling effects. For instance, when many people imagine a senior pastor, they picture a tall man whose race matches the congregation's majority. He probably has a resonant speaking voice and can work that church foyer meet-and-greet like nobody's business. None of those characteristics are negative, but for the many clergy who don't fit them, the existence of this archetype means they are subtly and not so subtly minimized, sidelined, or expected to squish into the mold.

Some of us encounter perceptions, like racism or sexism, that are against who God created us to be. Reginald Smith tells the story of his first day at a new church— a Black pastor of a majority-White, Reformed church in a majority-Hispanic neighborhood. When he knocked on the door, the custodian initially wouldn't let him in because he thought Smith was begging. When he finally opened the door to talk, he assumed Smith was asking for the pastor, not that he *was* the pastor. You may have had similar experiences where, in some core way, you were outside others' perceptions of your role, often in negative ways: "You're too pretty to be a pastor!" "Are you sure you're old enough?" "The students won't take you seriously." "You're too fat to sing lead." "Someone as quiet as you could never . . ."

Our fear of criticism shackles us to others' perceptions—or what we think others' perceptions might be if we were brave enough to live into our fullness. Part of this fear is rooted in reality. You don't want to be the target when a couple of influential board members get in a snit. So instead of bravely accepting God's gifts, you hunker down into the box you believe others see for you. Others could perceive your love of dressing well as prideful or self-absorbed, so you grow to think of it as such. You know you are a skilled speaker, but you don't lean into that gift because others might think you're showing off.

But we don't know how others will respond to our being fully ourselves, and only some criticism is valid. While being ourselves includes forethought about how our actions affect others, it doesn't make those perceptions our priority or assume they are accurate. Even though we care about others, we cannot control their perceptions of us and must not let those perceptions control us.

How then can we respond to others' perceptions and expectations of us, particularly the ones that don't lift us closer to Christ but weigh us down? First, we need to understand how we personally respond to expectations. Depending on our personalities, we may keenly feel a tension between our own selves and others' possible perceptions and misperceptions, even in the granular details of life. "If I do *this*, will I be bragging?" "If I share *that*, will people think I'm whining?" We may have a knee-jerk response to others' expectations or treat them as automatic obligations.

In her study of personality, Gretchen Rubin proposes that everyone responds to others' expectations, as well as their expectations of themselves, in one of four ways. First, as an "upholder," who typically finds it easy to meet both kinds of expectations. Second, as a "questioner," who follows the expectations that make sense to them and disregards the rest. Third, as an "obliger," who meets others' expectations (sometimes including ones that don't serve them or their values) but struggles to meet their inner expectations unless they find a source of external accountability, and as a result, may experience "obliger rebellion" and blow up against the external expectations.

Fourth, as a "rebel," who pushes against both their own and others' expectations, and instead finds motivation in their identity and their understanding of the positive and negative consequences for their choices.[3] These "four tendencies," as Rubin calls them, all have strengths and weaknesses. In ministry settings, we should be aware of how we respond to the outer expectations placed on us, especially since they often have little relationship to us personally and instead stem from others' experiences of Christianity and church dynamics.

Second, we must realistically understand what expectations and perceptions our neighbors tend to have. Though we can't erase every stereotype or rectify every inaccurate assumption, we can use our power to shape them and to choose how we respond. Adapting to some kinds of perceptions doesn't lead to creating a fake persona, because it comes from figuring out which one of our many facets—our many honest ways we can self-present—we might want to emphasize. "We can't control other people's perceptions, but we would be stupid to ignore them," says Nikki Toyama-Szeto, a nonprofit leader. Because she has realistically understood the assumptions many people make about her and her role, she can use those assumptions as a springboard for her goals. For instance, she intentionally uses stereotypes of Asian-American women leaders as nonthreatening people— "they're going to think I'm nervous, they're going think I am younger than I am, they're not going to think I'm the leader"—as an opportunity to ask "troubling and disruptive questions."

Similarly, homiletics professor Eunjoo Mary Kim leans into assumptions about her as a Korean woman when she teaches and preaches in the United States. She explains, "I had a different experience of my childhood, and the process of my spiritual formation is different from Americans, so people assume that I am different. Even in classes, I think students expect a different thing from me. I'm just free in many ways to express who I am and then also carry who I am into my teaching and my conversation."

We may choose to tolerate some misperceptions, especially superficial ones. Describing some of her conversations mentoring seminary students, Molly Baskette says, "I totally advocate for bodily autonomy. I totally advocate for self-expression. At the same time, I've also found myself saying a version of, 'If you want to be taken seriously, you really should think about not wearing a tube top leading worship.'" Presumably, the tube top or whatever is a relatively trivial choice, not one that's necessary to being yourself. So if congregants often assume you're a youth and not the youth leader, you might choose to consider others' perceptions and dress differently.

On the other hand, how we make these relatively trivial choices can reveal something deeper about what is truly integral to us. For instance, I swear, but not in most settings. I'm not hiding anything about myself by not saying something that could offend, but rather, I'm engaging in a context-appropriate behavior that points to something important that later chapters go into more closely: restraint is part of ministry but isn't the same as erasing who we are.

THE BIG (MIS)PERCEPTION

In conclusion, we need to consider one big perception—hopefully *mis*perception—that many people have about us as professional Christians: that we are hypocrites. They think this, not necessarily because of who we are as individuals, but because of everything discussed so far in this chapter. Because we are representatives, held to higher standards, have power, and are role models—and because of some people's past experiences with Christians (whether lay or leadership, in personal interactions or in media representations)—they carry a deep distrust of who we are.

You can probably think of Christian leaders you've encountered who give rise to this perception. I know I can, starting with my memories of being a kid playing piano up at the front of the sanctuary during altar calls—"every head bowed, every eye closed"—and occasionally hearing a preacher declare, "I see those hands," when there was not a single one raised. (Yes, it takes a special kind of hypocrisy to lie to the people of God, in the house of God, as a putative man of God, who's supposed to be preaching the word of God. Lord, have mercy.)

Most of us aren't hypocrites, and as professional Christians, we can begin to redress the problem—starting by being ourselves. Think back to how our ministry is enriched when we become more fully ourselves. Pastor Jude Harmon observes, "I think one of the biggest challenges that people have with church generally is that they associate it with hypocrisy and inauthenticity. The only way to get past that is to be *more* who we are, and to not present that we're something that we're not, even as we aspire to be something more than who we are." Being more fully ourselves comes across in many ways; for Harmon, it has included occasionally sharing his own experiences while preaching—experiences that connect with his ministry outside the sanctuary. "It does feel dangerous to let people in in that way," he tells me, "but if we don't, I think we miss the opportunity to connect and invite people to explore their own vulnerability and share their own witness."

Despite the complexity of being ourselves as professional Christians, God calls us to be ourselves—a reality that might relieve us as well as inspire us. "People want to know who they're dealing with, particularly when they're in a vulnerable place," Harmon says. "They want to know that they can trust people, and to do that, they do have to hear something about who you actually are." Imagine that: ministry by being fully who we are, and no less.

KEY TAKEAWAYS

Several factors complicate how we can be fully ourselves in public ministry. First, we represent faith to many people, a reality that can be jarring if our training didn't prepare us. Second, many of us have relational power, such as the power to influence others. Third, our communities often elevate us as role models while also holding us to high moral standards, a position that allows us to be role models of failure, forgiveness, and grace.

Finally, our various ministry roles are part of who we are. These roles are not a layer on top of our "true" identities but are integral to our whole selves. We must be aware of others' (mis)perceptions while not being controlled by them.

DISCUSSION QUESTIONS

1. How is your experience of being a professional Christian different from that of people who aren't

professional Christians or from your experiences before becoming a professional Christian?

2. Do people in your branch of Christianity see you as a representative of the faith? How does that affect your interactions with them?

3. What do you think about your role in influencing people? Do you experience obligation? Have you encountered any pitfalls that come with being influential? What do you intentionally do as a role model?

4. How is your ministry role part of who you are? What gaps or liminal space do you feel in that role?

5. What (mis)perceptions do you repeatedly encounter? How do you tend to respond? How might you respond differently?

Chapter 3

AUTHENTICITY, SINCERITY, AND OTHER WAYS TO IMAGINE HOW TO BE OURSELVES

Part of the difficulty of being fully ourselves in the spotlight of public ministry is that we use a wealth of imperfect metaphors to get at what we mean. We use words like *authenticity* and *sincerity* to talk about heartfelt self-expression and phrases like "wearing hats" to imagine what being ourselves can look like in different situations. Each concept falls short of capturing the vast humanity implied in *being ourselves*. (How unsurprising that we can't cram our fully human, fully made-in-God's-image selves into a neat conceptual package!) Sometimes our concepts do more harm than good, as commercialism and even hucksterism gum up something that seems as if it should be intuitive. Some of our concepts express goals whose flaws pose significant detriments to ourselves and our ministries. At the same time, each brings its own assets that collectively form a helpful picture.

Since our language profoundly shapes our self-understanding and our perception of the world, this chapter examines the verbal concepts shaping our lives—the "metaphors we live by," as cognitive linguists George Lakoff and Mark Johnson put it—to get at what being ourselves can mean.[1] We will start with *authenticity*, a tangle of a concept if there ever was one, but a concept brimming with insights into self-expression. Then we'll consider what *sincerity* and *persona* can teach us about being ourselves while acting appropriately to our circumstances. Finally, we'll end with *vulnerability* as the thread tying the chapter together. Whether or not we realize it, these concepts continually inform how we understand ourselves and our relationships, so they are worth examining as part of our pursuit to live thoughtful, faith-filled lives as professional Christians.

Something important might get lost in this labyrinth, so I want to emphasize it now. In the words of pastor Brian Erickson, "We can't get so hung up on our authenticity that we're presenting ourselves more than we're presenting the Gospel." Similarly, M.R., a priest, explains that "striving for the best version of myself as a minister has to be rooted in that striving to stay close to Jesus," that is, in being "authentic to Jesus Christ." Our desires to be fully ourselves must come down to the question: to what or to whom are we being true? Ultimately, we must be true to Jesus and the Gospel.

THE THICKET OF AUTHENTICITY

Authenticity looms largest in our concepts of what it is to be ourselves, especially given its popularity in Christian spaces. Its most basic meaning is *being true to yourself*, a meaning that frequently gets expanded to become *being true to your spontaneous feelings*. Yet as professional Christians, we often can't and shouldn't act on our gut impulses. Are we then inauthentic, with all the negativity that word implies?

To explore the answers to that question, we need to examine this convoluted concept's numerous denotative and connotative meanings. Some turn on the light for our self-understanding, while some express values and goals that are harmful to ourselves and our ministries. (There is a reason "authenticity" isn't on the cover of this book, even though I've used it plenty of times to describe the topic.)

Part of what makes authenticity tricky as a concept is that it has a good/bad dichotomy baked into it—that is, we understand it as "this good thing" *in contrast to* "this bad thing." As a dictionary would define authenticity as it relates to people, authenticity means *being true to your origins or group*, in contrast to being pretentious or selling out. Second, authenticity means *being self-realized or self-actualized*, in contrast to hiding integral aspects of yourself or being ignorant of them entirely. This dichotomy can look like talking about "authentic worship" by setting it up against whatever the inauthentic (and therefore bad) worship is, or declaring our way (or our church's way) to be the authentic/good one, unlike whatever "fake" thing other Christians are doing.

Adding to the complexity is that authenticity is also a way to brand commodities. We talk about authentic restaurants, authentic jeans, and, yes, authentic spirituality, all defined in contrast to the inauthentic version. Advertisers capitalize on our desire to be ourselves by selling us the false promise that somehow this shirt, this vacation, this church service could make us more ourselves—as if an exchange of money or time could reveal our truest colors. As if!

Finally, we can't forget how often authenticity is framed as a value in Christian circles, especially through the branding of churches and faith-related commodities. We certainly want our faith to be authentic in the sense of being true, but as I mentioned in the introduction, I find our common use of authenticity to be problematic. First, because of its close relationship with coolness and trying to make Jesus and following him cool. Second, because of authenticity's frequent usage to mean *being true to your spontaneous feelings.* While it's not always a problem to immediately express our inner state, we often shouldn't do this: God calls us to curb sinful impulses; to be discrete, wise, and temperate; and to love our neighbors regardless of whatever we might feel at the moment.

To help us understand how authenticity can be both a positive and negative attribute to aspire to, let's go back to the eighteenth century, with the argument that authenticity is our natural state. We'll start there and then walk a full circle through authenticity's connotative thicket.

Authenticity as Naturalness

The father of our modern authenticity concept is the French Enlightenment-era philosopher and composer Jean-Jacques Rousseau. For Rousseau and his followers, authenticity is a person's natural condition, as they express their spontaneous, of-the-moment feelings. Planning our behaviors, intentionally curating our self-presentation, and even being diplomatic are antithetical to this understanding of authenticity. Professional ethics and behavior also clash with this connotation's values: the physician's gut response to a horrifying physical condition is the authentic one, while their professional care is a false courtesy, a denial of reality. Being a professional doesn't mean denying our own feelings, but it often means delaying their expression until an appropriate time and place, in contrast to the immediacy of *authenticity as naturalness.*

Authenticity as naturalness feels fundamentally immature and self-centered in many situations (the therapist had better not gasp when we reveal a deep secret), but the scenarios we professional Christians encounter frequently prioritize this kind of authenticity, such as in church services and pastoral-care settings. When we expect leading musicians and preachers to be *authentically worshiping* in a church service, we put them in a bind of either *actually* worshiping or else putting on a false front of what "worship" looks like to our particular congregation. In the either/or of Rousseauian authenticity, when an exhausted musician enthusiastically leads the congregation's singing, they are necessarily inauthentic, that is, lying to God and their neighbors. Similarly, when a preacher praises God while also in a season of despair, they are inauthentic in the Rousseauian sense. There is no good third way, no escape hatch from Rousseau's model.

Authenticity as Artistic Expression

As we continue thinking about what musicians and other worship leaders must do to be authentic during the act of leading church services, let's use the lens of *authenticity as artistic expression,* where we convey our personhood through the art we make. In this connotation, authentic art must express something true about its creator.

In many traditions, worship leaders' goals have little to do with personal expression. Like a lector whose reading of Isaiah may say a lot about God and little or nothing about the lector personally, these leaders are outside the framework of *authenticity as artistic expression.* But in many other traditions, leaders are expected to artistically express their hearts when they preach or sing solos. It's not just that they must sing words the congregation believes are true, that they must preach a sermon in accordance with their denomination's theology, or even that they must personally believe in whatever they are saying. Their preaching and singing must convey something true about them *as artistic creators.*

This value on *authenticity as artistic expression* does not make room for personal ups and downs or the times when the personal vulnerability implied in this kind of authenticity is not necessary or desirable. Like the concept of *authenticity as naturalness, authenticity as artistic expression* has no good third way, no space for play, no break from its unrelenting self-consciousness, and ignores how God can work through a sermon that is more college lecture than personal account or a vocal solo that says practically nothing personally expressive about the singer.

Authenticity as Moral Relativism

Because one of authenticity's denotative meanings is being self-realized or self-actualized, authenticity may connotatively imply moral relativism. What is good and true for me may not be good and true for you; there is no objectively right path, only what is right for me at this moment. The cosmos-sized arguments about moral relativism in our Christian circles all beg this question about authenticity: is self-realization primarily a good impulse or not?

How we answer the question—and whether each of us views *authenticity as moral relativism* positively or negatively—depends on how we understand human nature.

On one hand, many Christians can positively view self-realization as a form of being more and more conformed to the image of Christ, a process bringing us closer to how God made us to be. As I put it in the introduction, being closer to God makes us more truly ourselves, that is, more self-realized.

On the other hand, many Christians believe people are fundamentally marred, sinful, fallen. From this perspective, no one should desire complete self-realization. Some

Christians would even argue we can't truly know the depths of our depravity—"The heart is deceitful above all things, and desperately wicked" (Jer. 17:9 KJV)—so we certainly shouldn't plumb those depths in a misguided pursuit of authenticity. For those with this view, *authenticity as moral relativism* is yet another connotation with dubious value.

Authenticity as Provenance

Authenticity's other denotative meaning is being true to one's origins, which brings us to *authenticity as provenance*, one of the more important and valuable ways of thinking about authenticity for ministry leaders.

Provenance means where something or someone came from. In the world of art and antiques, we may say a painting is "an authentic El Greco" to mean the painting is in the definitive oeuvre of the artist. While we cannot always be sure (some art is very old, and some forgeries are very good), we recognize the artist painted a finite number of works, and each painting's provenance is authentic in this sense.

Our primary concern, though, is people. For people, provenance is much trickier. Take someone from the backwoods who took a gap year in Europe and came back with a new accent, never to acknowledge their rural roots again. Most of us would see that behavior as inauthentic, or at the least complicated—and we don't mean complicated in a good way.

But what about the person whose accent differs in a work or social setting from when phoning home? We probably wouldn't use the authentic/inauthentic dichotomy to understand this scenario at all and instead would compare it to the verbal differences we show between talking to five-year-olds and talking to adults. (For those who believe we should speak the same to children and adults: one, I hope this book expands your perspective, and two, please don't swear around my language-sponge toddler. Being *that* parent is not a goal of mine.)

Here's a scenario that hits closer to home for us professional Christians. Our profession springs from our faith, that is, our spiritual origins. Because of our faith/origins, we can make a living. Put bluntly, we make money from our faith. That money, combined with the power of our positions, can become a barrier in our ministries. If we become disconnected from our origins or if people perceive a disconnect (regardless of reality), we cannot minister as effectively.

Most of us in ministry aren't particularly wealthy or famous, but we are culturally powerful compared to many in our organizations. We tend to be well educated; people listen when we speak; and even if our income is barely middle-class, our churches usually include many people without even that level of economic comfort. But our ministry is grounded—must be grounded—in faith.

How can we show that we are true to our faith origins? We must often ask ourselves that question as our circumstances evolve over the years. We must stay grounded and remind ourselves that even if *we* feel connected to our origins, *authenticity as provenance* is also in the eye of the beholder. As explored in the previous chapter, we cannot control others' (mis)perceptions, but we shouldn't discount them either.

Authenticity as Commodity

We can purchase "authentic" things: authentic clothing, authentic travel destinations, authentic food. The promise is certainly appealing: wouldn't being ourselves be much easier if we could buy it (not easier for the poorer among us, but nice for those who can afford it)?

We can buy two kinds of authenticity: the "real authentic" and the "fake authentic" (that is, the inauthentic thing someone claims is authentic). Typically, we find "real authentic" at higher prices: the Italian-tasting menu created by an Italian chef versus the chain restaurant claiming to be like Nona's. Even if the jeans I'm wearing claim to be "authentic," they're "fake authentic" because they aren't work clothes, as "real authentic" jeans would be.

Here's the problem with *authenticity as commodity*, according to philosopher Andrew Potter. Regardless of whether you've bought a "fake authentic" or "real authentic" product, what you've bought is a status symbol.[2] Both kinds of authentic purchases rely on comparing our authentic/good stuff with the fake/bad stuff our neighbors have (and, in case it wasn't obvious, Christianity is against buying things to make ourselves seem better than our neighbors). We're back to the good/bad dichotomy that's part of authenticity's core meaning.

The problem isn't wanting to look good, but wanting to look better than others. The problem isn't wanting a church service that comes from a heart of faith, but thinking our church's ability to purchase the latest tech or hire that great preacher has anything to do with expressing that heart. The problem isn't wanting a website that accurately reflects our school's constituents, but treating that commodity as a sign that our school is more authentic than another school that can afford only a basic website. This kind of authenticity is problematic because jockeying for status is antithetical to Christianity, not because we care about making the church service or website as good as we can.

It's a tangled situation, especially since, as Erickson points out, many people in ministry "so want to be relevant, so want to be cool, even though in their secular lives they're neither cool nor relevant." (After all, "we didn't get into this work because we were captain of the football team," he notes). On one hand, we want to be ourselves, that is, to be personally authentic. On the other hand, we will gain status if we can achieve the impression that we are being ourselves, especially if being ourselves involves a hint of coolness (the coolness coming from several kinds of authenticity, including commodity, naturalness, provenance, and artistic expression). Understandably we might want that higher status because it has tangible benefits, such as being more likely to be hired if we seem authentic. So we may be tempted to try to purchase our way into that flavor of authenticity.

On the outside, the difference isn't apparent. We cannot see others' hearts, and they cannot see ours. Even if we think we can spot someone else buying status symbols, our perceptions may be clouded by jealousy or insecurity. Discerning our personal motivations here can be incredibly difficult as well. So we have to come back to the Gospel and our ultimate goal of being authentic to Jesus Christ as we follow him, and then discern our motivations in conversation with trusted counselors and friends.

Authenticity as Actuality

You may notice a recurring trend among all the meanings of authenticity so far: we often use "authentic" to mean "actual." In other words, we use "authentic" as a redundant adjective. There is no such thing as "authentic faith," but faith, unbelief, and the vast terrain between those, where most of us journey. There is no such thing as "authentic worship," but worship and the path leading to and from it. If I remind myself, "Be authentically Sarah," what I mean is, "Be Sarah." *Be myself.*

Authenticity as Return

We've made our way through the thicket of authenticity and circled back to Rousseau. His formulation of *authenticity as naturalness* connects inextricably to the last connotation of authenticity: *authenticity as return*, the belief that once upon a time we existed in some unfallen, unspoiled state.

Yes, authenticity as Eden.

Frequently this form of authenticity comes commercially packaged as a way "back to our roots." Back to an earlier musical style, back to the Nicene Creed, back to the Bible, and so on. If it's old, it must be good, right?

As Christians, we may imagine a positive spin on this kind of authenticity: we come from God and must return to God to be our truest selves. But we may also see the dangers of imagining that Christians in the first century were somehow "closer" to God than we could ever be. That archaic language must be holier. That the mothers and fathers of the church have something that we cannot experience. That older times were simpler times, better times.

Focusing on the good aspects of the past can blind us to its evils and cause us to fear the possibilities of the present, instead of following the Spirit's leading in the tools of our own cultures and times.

SINCERITY: A MIDDLE GROUND

Sincerity is situated close to its conceptual cousin, authenticity, but leans away from self-expression and toward being ourselves in different settings. Like authenticity, sincerity has many definitions with subtle differences in meaning. Generally speaking, though, when we talk about being sincere, we mean *being who you say you are*, or conversely, *not being a hypocrite.* There are three important aspects of sincerity as it relates to being ourselves as professional Christians. Here's the key to them all: sincerity teaches us that being ourselves doesn't necessarily involve *all* of us, *all* the time.

First, from the *Oxford English Dictionary*, "sincerity" means "containing no element of dissimulation or deception; not feigned or pretended." In this sense, being sincere about yourself means that you are not intentionally lying or intentionally hiding yourself. It does *not* mean you are being deliberately self-expressive or trying to live as your fullest self. Many of us treat this aspect of sincerity as our highest personal goal as we relate our inner selves to others: No lying or pretending. The end.

Second, from the literary critic Lionel Trilling in his influential work *Sincerity and Authenticity*, is another way of thinking about sincerity, through three components: "communication without deceiving or misleading"; "a single-minded commitment to whatever dutiful enterprise [one] may have in hand"; and being "oneself, in action, [and] in deeds."[3] This sincerity is about intent: we can misunderstand ourselves or our circumstances and be both sincere and wrong. This sincerity is not the same as being self-expressive, and it is not about living out our deepest desires: I can be sincere in my daily life while also thinking, "But I always wanted to be an artist."

This formulation of sincerity gives us a positive way of understanding professionalism, especially when we have distressing experiences ministering to people who have come to us because they can expect a professional response, not our gut reaction. Our actions are not necessarily inferior if they are not authentic. For instance, my husband, a physician, once described his *authentic as natural* response to a medical emergency ("It was like a horror movie"), coupled with his sincere, professional response ("I didn't need to do chest compressions because I wasn't on the Code Team"). To paraphrase Trilling, we can see through the lens of sincerity how to be ourselves in actions and deeds while living into the "dutiful enterprise" of our ministry to others.

Third, Trilling brings up another way to view sincerity, which includes "confrontation of what is base or shameful in oneself."[4] We rarely use this sense of sincerity in Anglo circles (it comes from a French tradition), but it's one of the most important aspects of being ourselves for professional Christians. The clear sight of sincerity can keep us from undue pride and from imagining we are better than our neighbors. By being aware of our shortcomings, hopefully we gain compassion for others' flaws.

Moving away from authenticity and sincerity, let's take the rest of this chapter to learn what *persona* can teach us about being ourselves in different settings.

HOW CAN WE BE FULLY OURSELVES IN DIFFERENT SITUATIONS?

Part of being ourselves includes self-expression, and another important aspect of being ourselves is how we act in different circumstances. It's all well and good to be self-expressive, but often we're in situations where self-expression is low on the priority list or in scenarios where the diplomacy required appears at odds with being ourselves.

To make the situation even more complicated, think of the word "act," as in, "How do I *act* in different circumstances?" "Act" here is used in the sense of behavior, but the metaphor of acting is also deeply embedded in how we understand the strange and empathetic ways we relate to other people as they need us to relate and communicate so they can hear us.

Our relationships with others throughout our lives are ripe for an acting metaphor. Shakespeare famously used this in *As You Like It*: "All the world's a stage, / And all the men and women merely players; / They have their exits and their entrances, / And one man in his time plays many parts, / His acts being seven ages."[5] More recently, twentieth-century sociologist Erving Goffman proposed that a person *is like* an actor throughout their life, and literary theorist Kenneth Burke took the metaphor further, arguing instead that a person *is* an actor in their life.

Apt as it is, the metaphor of acting may feel like a poor fit for professional Christians. Saying that we're "acting" feels false, as if we're putting on a front and behaving in ways that aren't true to who we are or what we believe. Nonetheless, we shouldn't miss the fact that we are like actors whenever we wisely consider our interactions. Like an actor, we care about how our communication affects others and how others perceive us (and practically everyone cares about how they're perceived, except for some saints, "fools for Christ," and sociopaths).

Let's stay with this acting metaphor for a while, in the form of *persona*, to see what it can teach about being ourselves in various settings. Like authenticity, persona's flaws—and the discomfort we may feel about "acting"—still generate valuable insights.

At its simplest, persona is an actor's role or a person's role in various social settings. As I'm using it here, persona is a way to understand how we present ourselves to other people, especially when communicating publicly through different media. (Each medium might have a different persona. You could say I have a writer persona, a podcaster persona, a preacher persona. Each sounds slightly different from each other, to accommodate various intended audiences and the norms of different media.) Though persona doesn't help us imagine our self-expression as authenticity does, persona provides us a way to talk about remaining fully integrated as our whole selves while navigating different situations where we may act in different ways.

Masks and Hats

Persona originally referred to theatrical masks worn by Roman actors, hence today's metaphorical meaning for the term: *how you present yourself to other people.* Today in English, we say something similar when we talk about wearing hats for different roles in our lives or wearing a mask to protect ourselves in difficult situations. From the perspective of these metaphors, we remain whole, integrated people, wearing whatever hat or mask our situation requires, regardless of our changing circumstances, the roles we take on, and the media we use to communicate.

The mask metaphor feels problematic, since "putting on a mask" is essentially a dishonest act. A mask covers our face, our most emotive body part. It purposely hides something, and that something is the spontaneity of *authenticity as naturalness.* Perhaps we are in a context where we ought to and even must conceal our of-the-moment feelings to remain professional, a situation where we should not wear our emotions on our shoulders, much less our faces. Frankly, temporarily donning a professional mask may protect the ones we serve from our gut responses.

Often the mask functions as a glossy cover for an imperfect reality, which is why this metaphor doesn't sit well for professional Christians. Our word *hypocrite* comes from the ancient Greek term for an actor, that is, "an interpreter from underneath" a mask. To live life always with a mask on is perpetual hypocrisy. It means never coming to terms with what *is*, never living into the powerful force of taking off the mask.

On the other hand, the hat metaphor can help us conceptualize our approach to ministry in different settings, especially ones where our own emotions don't match those of the people we serve. For example, pastor Lydia Sohn describes putting on her "minister hat" and then getting out "a set of tools that I use to help people work through difficult emotions." This metaphor allows for a healthy way of conceptualizing distinct roles and gives us a way to understand how some people see us primarily as representatives of a role (e.g., they may see us wearing our "professor hat" and associate us with that role alone). Wearing hats can be a healthier alternative to wearing masks, since a hat plops on our head without concealing our face. A hat stays for a little while, then is replaced by a new one. Certainly the concept can help us understand how to be ourselves—with our own emotions—while ministering to people in their own complex emotional spaces.

Yet both metaphors lack conceptual depth or nuance. How do I feel about these hats and masks? Did I select them myself? Do they signal to other people who I truly am? Most importantly, are they mere costume props, something I add and subtract to my truest self, but not reflections of who I am? A child may wear different hats all day, but they are not a cowboy, a chef, or a firefighter. Practically nothing about the costume reveals the child's inner self. At the end of the day, the child goes home, and the hats return to the cupboard, ready for a different child's play tomorrow.

Star Persona (Yes, We Have One, Even If We Aren't "Stars")

The metaphors of masks and hats lead us to a specific problem for public ministry. Whether in live events like corporate worship or through other media like writing, we step into roles that are somewhat apart from our everyday selves. In these roles of speaker, preacher, musician, and so on, people may believe we are "personally expressive"; that is, they think we are expressing our "real" selves as we lead them in song or as we read a Scripture passage.[6] But while we *may* be personally expressive at those times, we also have *star personas*. (Those of us who sing first-person solos—"I love God" songs, as opposed to ones with texts in the second and third person—simultaneously have *star* personas as well as *song* personas, that is, the persona of the first person "I" in the song's lyrics.) You may wonder how a small-town teacher can have a star persona. Isn't that for pop stars and possibly megachurch pastors? But public roles come with star personas, regardless of how famous we are.

Star personas are not about "being a star" but about being known in mediated ways. People know us through social media platforms, through public speaking, through something as simple as posting sermon recordings on the internet. We can now be "known" without any other context or in-person connection. We also gain star persona through interpersonal interactions where we are in power, especially when we have access to far more information than the people we serve. In all these scenarios, people see a slice of us—our star persona—without seeing the whole, and any "relationship" is a one-sided, parasocial one, not one founded in reciprocal friendship.

Here's an example. In a prerecorded worship service during the COVID-19 pandemic, a snippet of extra video snuck past the editor. Instead of starting with me introducing a new song, the section began with me adjusting my scarf, looking into the camera, freezing a smile for a couple of seconds, then finally launching into the song.

What were those extra five seconds? A distraction? The "real me" before Sarah the Music Minister took over? An unintended "behind the scenes"? As I see it, those moments were a reminder that I am known in mediated ways and that there is more to me than the slice people usually see.

Having a star persona isn't intrinsically good or bad. It's simply a factor we need to keep in mind as we minister publicly, since most people won't think of us as having one (unless we are ridiculously famous). Unless something intervenes, like the extra video footage, most people will not perceive our roles of preacher, teacher, worship leader, and so on as *roles* ("It's just Sarah, up there leading music," not "Sarah-the-Minister-of-Music leading music").

That's the rub. We *do* have roles in our various ministries, and we *do* think carefully about what we share and what we don't. But the people we minister to often perceive us as only ourselves, with no thoughtful mediation between us.

The way we can access private spaces and daily lives on social media adds to the illusion. Previously, you might never see my office unless you knew me personally. But now, when you follow me online, you'll eventually see a picture of my messy desk. The problem (if there is a problem) isn't sharing a photo of my office online. The problem is the illusion that you *know* me because you've seen what I share publicly, even though we've never met or even though we know each other only through my ministry in the church. Friendship—knowing—is a two-way relationship, but social media can surely make us feel as if we know someone when we see only one facet of them. Their star persona is not fake, but it's only one part of the whole.

By understanding that we have star personas, even if our audiences don't always realize this, we can be more thoughtful about our signaling. As professional Christians, our ministries are no longer limited to face-to-face interactions on a Sunday morning, our street clothes covered in liturgical garb. We can both minister in our local setting and reach out beyond it. With wisdom and God's help, our star personas can aid our ministries instead of muddling them.

Alter Egos: The Overflowing of Personality

You may have read this whole section on persona and wondered when I would bring up *alter egos* (or "altar egos," as they are called where ministry leaders are concerned).[7] After all, alter egos are probably the most common mode of talking about persona. Plus, alter egos help us think about what our self-expression in various contexts could look like.

Alter egos are about personality overflowing one brand or reputation. The everyday persona cannot contain the multitude and magnificence of a whole person, and so another— the alter ego—is created. In the popular imagination, the alter ego is usually wilder, bigger, bolder than the "everyday" persona—think of Clark Kent and Superman, Bruce Wayne and Batman. Even the comic book character Calvin, already a force in and of himself, bursts out with many outsize alter egos like Spaceman Spiff.

An alter ego also can be a relatively tame way to imagine better versions of ourselves. Sometimes I coax myself into tedious but necessary work by telling myself, "Okay, I will hire myself as my administrative assistant for the next hour," and then blast through a bunch of work I wish I could hire out. Similarly, we may say, "I will be like So-and-so," and name a kind friend as we strive to act in ways we believe we should.

But there is nothing integrated or whole about having an alter ego. Instead, we should live into our whole selves *as ourselves*, no alter ego needed. When we *do* act kindly, it's *us* doing the kind action. (And sadly, it's just me answering my emails.)

Troubling as an alter ego is, alter egos have something important to teach us as we align our actions with our values. We need to be aware that alter egos are a way of coping with our circumstances, especially when we feel disempowered. They are a warning signal of our feeling compelled to act out in ways radically different from our norm by constructing an alternative identity or environment that's bigger and bolder than our reality. We may not be able to change immediately, but listening to our desire for an alter ego can prompt us to build a bigger life where our whole, integrated self can flourish.

ON VULNERABILITY AND MULTIFACETED GEMS

Authenticity, sincerity, and persona are flawed concepts, yet full of insights into what being ourselves can be, both in terms of self-expression and shaping our behavior to different settings. To round out our exploration, I want to leave you with two more ways to imagine how to be ourselves.

Let's start with *vulnerability*. Vulnerability means being exposed to emotional or physical harm. It means taking off the emotional mask, taking off the armor, and letting ourselves be open to the flourishing of relationship and open to betrayal. Open to unalloyed joy and open to heartbreak.

Vulnerability is ever present in our ministries. When we release something we've created into the world, we're opening ourselves up to whatever responses may come. Every time we preach a sermon, sing a solo, or write an essay, we're vulnerable to some extent or another, because we're opening ourselves up to the "uncertainty, risk, and emotional exposure" that researcher Brené Brown sees at the core of vulnerability.[8]

Though vulnerability is about openness, it is not about self-disclosure. In defining vulnerability, Brown makes the point that it is not the same as sharing personal stories purely to get eyeballs on you.[9] (Consider that loving someone enough that they could hurt you doesn't necessarily mean you've shared every detail about yourself with them.)

Even though we're being vulnerable by sharing our creations with others, we share only a fraction of ourselves as we do so. Here's a helpful metaphor: imagine a person as a multifaceted gem that enfleshes the common phrase "facets of personality." A person is like a multifaceted gem that is so big that others can see only a facet or two at a time. Perhaps a few people have developed such deep and robust relationships that they can see nearly the whole gem. But no one is the gem except the gem itself, and no one else can truly understand the whole of the gem except the one who is the gem.

You are that gem—that big, beautiful person made by God.

Everyone around you can see your facets—a glimpse here, a thirty-minute conversation there. Some people become close, and a few come close enough to seemingly see all of you. But still they see you only from the outside, and only you are the fullest self.

Thinking of yourself as a multifaceted gem frees you to bring what's useful and healthy to a specific setting, since, as pastor Bethany McKinney Fox points out, you "don't need to bring every single facet to every single environment or interaction." This perspective can bring you joy and fulfillment as you explore your various facets in different settings, instead of limiting yourself.

This perspective can also help you integrate what might seem like disparate aspects of your personal or professional identity. For example, Braxton Shelley is a professor as well as a minister and musician. He describes his integration of these professions as a "rotation" where he puts the spotlight or "intensity" on one area but always brings them all to the table, since the synthesis of the three is what makes him distinctive.

Like Fox and Shelley, you have your own distinct constellation of gifts, expertise, and personality. By thinking about everything that makes you *you* as the facets of a gem, you can see how showing only a part of yourself is still showing *you*. You can discern what you want to share (or not) in ways that don't feel like hiding but like acknowledging the reality of your bigness.

✳ ✳ ✳

KEY TAKEAWAYS

We have many concepts and metaphors for being fully ourselves. Authenticity is a slippery, often problematic way to express being truly and fully ourselves, even if it is the most common. *Authenticity as naturalness*—where we express our spontaneous, of-the-moment feelings—is a frequent meaning and is fundamentally immature.

Sincerity, *being who you say you are*, is a positive way of understanding professional behavior that doesn't line up with our gut emotions.

Persona and metaphors of masks and hats are ways to talk about remaining fully integrated while navigating situations where we may act in different ways. At the same time, their connotations of acting in a fake way highlight the pitfall of hypocrisy.

Vulnerability and the metaphor of a multifaceted gem give us ways to think about being fully ourselves, even when other people cannot see all of us.

DISCUSSION QUESTIONS

1. What connotations does "authenticity" have for you?
2. When have you experienced a clash between *authenticity as naturalness* and your need for professionalism?
3. Have you ever purchased something "authentic" to gain status? Did it help?
4. Where does sincerity fit in your understanding of being a professional?
5. What does it mean for you to have a star persona, even if most others don't realize it?
6. What do you think about alter egos as coping strategies?
7. How does the metaphor of a multifaceted gem resonate with you?

Chapter 4

COMMUNICATING WITH NEIGHBORS WE KNOW—AND THOSE WE DON'T

Who are our neighbors, especially if we can't see them? Given the many options we have for communication these days, how do we talk with the people we minister to, both the ones we know and the ones who are practically anonymous? How do we prevent or mitigate miscommunications?

We can't begin to answer these questions without thinking about who *we* are to each neighbor, because the relationship shapes who we are and who that neighbor is. We can't be fully ourselves apart from other people. I can't be *Sarah* without my relationships like *Wife, Daughter, Friend,* and so on. For most of these relationships, I know exactly which people I'm in relationship with: Brandon, Lee, Crawford, and so on. I know not only which people I'm in relationship with; I know *who I am* in relationship with them. I am *Lee's Daughter* just as much as she is *Sarah's Mother.* (This is true not just with our earthly relationships. There is no *me* to be outside of relationship with God. I am not *Sarah* without being *God's Child.*)

However, for my looser relationships, especially ones that aren't in person, I often have little idea whom I'm in relationship with. Take my relationship with you, the reader. You may think that this isn't a relationship, because you have never spoken with me before, but think of this book as an opening gambit to a conversation I am inviting you to continue. In this perspective, you and I are in relationship, albeit loosely, and thus we are neighbors. My intention is a readership of ministry leaders, so I'm writing to you with that assumption about who you are. But really I don't know anything about you except that you read English and are interested in this book's topic. Yet here I am, communicating with you all the same.

To echo Jesus' parable of the Good Samaritan, Who is a neighbor? The one who chooses relationship with the people they encounter. In today's world, we may consider both closer and looser relationships part of being neighbors. Perhaps our neighborhoods are any communities in which we are communicating, like an online group we are part of, a conference we attend, or a meeting of our local worship leaders. This chapter considers the difficulty and potentials of communication in our modern age, starting with that seemingly simple question: Who is my neighbor?

BEING NEIGHBORS TO STRANGERS

To share the Gospel so our neighbors can hear, we must know who our neighbors are, then communicate with them as best we can. We are never communicating with everyone, so when we are being ourselves, we are being ourselves in relationship with specific people. This specificity may make sense in closer relationships, but what does that mean for looser relationships? What is our responsibility to love people whom we don't know well or at all?

Complicating the issue is that our more distant neighbors may think they know us better than they do, because of the illusion of a closer relationship that some media, especially social media, give. Although our use of social media can provide a sense of personal proximity, our communication on those platforms is as curated as any other public medium we use. Other people may think they see the whole story when they are getting only one slice of our lives, just as they may not realize we have a star persona.

In our virtual age, it's easy to lose sight of our more distant neighbors, but in the past the connection between our medium and our neighbors was nearly always self-evident. Think of how it was only fifty years ago. Some people communicated to large audiences of strangers, but your average professional Christian didn't have that kind of reach. Mostly, they spoke with the people they knew. Why talk about navigating various media's forms and functions when seemingly everyone knows the difference between a phone conversation with their aunt and a public address to their denominational colleagues? Why ask who your neighbor is, when you can see them face to face on the sidewalk?

When we think of our neighbors as folks in the pews, it's easy to realize that *of course they are people, of course they are our neighbors.* However, when we move beyond the limited reach of our specific location—our nonprofit's office, this semester's enrolled students—sometimes our neighbors lose their faces and become a throng of strangers. One of the great illusions of our time is that when we communicate through virtual media like websites and podcasts, we have an endless, unknowable audience, and instead of speaking to discrete individuals, we are speaking into a void. While it is technically accurate that billions of people could visit a website, it's not the reality. Our neighborhoods, both physical and virtual, are relatively small, and even the most popular of us, the one with the loudest megaphone, doesn't have some unknowable following.

When we put our minds to it, we can tell whom we're reaching, at least their general contours. Maybe you've noticed people who communicate with this knowledge in mind, whether through virtual or physical media. Musician Adán Fernández tells me it's as if he is speaking to a specific person while letting others listen in on the conversation. Sometimes he even lets others "in on the joke." This is a stark contrast with how people communicate when they think they have to shout at a blank wall. Fernández knows who his neighbors are, even when he is communicating virtually. Sure, he can't see specifically who every single person is in his audience, and neither can we; but we do have a good sense of who they are or can find out with a little research.

Yes, all I truly know about you, the reader, is that you can read English and are interested in this book's topic. But I know that you, my neighbor, with few exceptions, are a Christian leader who cares about ministering with your whole heart.

WHICH NEIGHBORS ARE WE TALKING WITH?

Since we can reach such a wide range of neighbors, we need to consider our intended audience when we speak up. Maria McDowell contrasts how she has talked about racism on her blog, where she assumes a mostly White audience, with her sermons at the historically Black church she pastors. The content is different—"I don't need to teach people in my congregation about racism"—and so is the relationship. She isn't the pastor of her blog audience, but she is the pastor of the people she preaches to.

We also need to consider potential reach beyond our intended audience, especially when using media that are easily reproducible. We're preaching not only to the people in front of us but to listeners of a live broadcast. We're not only writing letters that are relatively difficult to share but are sending emails that recipients can forward with a single click. We can choose to communicate with these facts in mind. (By "communicate with these facts in mind," I certainly do not mean sending a passive-aggressive message to one person by broadcasting a public social-media message. Just in case you were wondering.)

Finally, we need to consider what our relationship is to the people we are communicating with. For instance, when McDowell considered who her audience was, she wasn't just noticing "blog audience" or "congregation," but that she was in the relationship of *pastor* to the latter group. It's an especially important evaluation to make for people who preach and who engage in pastoral care. If you were a guest preacher, your lack of rapport with the congregation would inform your preaching. But if you were preaching at your home church, you would be preaching mostly to people who have a long-standing relationship with you. Now imagine that you are that same preacher—the one who pastors, the one who sometimes guest preaches—and you are speaking to people through a virtual medium. Some of the people you are talking with are parishioners, but many are not. How then do you communicate? What is your standing to speak pastorally?

The differences here are vital in discussing complex and controversial issues, something that chapter 6 addresses in fuller detail. Speaking about something controversial to our congregation or classroom is different than saying the same thing to a constellation of high school classmates, colleagues, second cousins, and random folks we've never even met. Educator Casey Stanton points out that, for this specific reason, she doesn't use social media to talk about controversial topics: "I'm just much more comfortable being honest and taking risks in real relationships that I can see and touch, with people I am accountable to and sharing life with." On the other hand, professor Tanya Riches takes a different approach. She intentionally uses social media to connect with a wide range of people, often on controversial issues. She explains, "I'm not simply marketing a church. I'm doing ministry. I'm doing things that I see as a vocation."

Pastor and professor Will Willimon draws out this distinction in our relationships. Speaking to people as their pastor is "different than making a statement in the newspaper or going on Facebook, because I don't really have the credentials there. There, I'm just somebody spouting off about my opinion. But at church, I'm a pastor, and I'm preaching to my folk." The closer relationship, often with a history of pastoral care, allows for a different conversation about complex topics.

Nevertheless, virtual relationships can have a pastoral element in some situations. Minister and writer Lydia Sohn points out that in virtual spaces, she can't personally connect with each person—a factor that may feel like a loss but that is also part of the benefit of using different media. "The larger the following, the harder it is for me to connect with every single person. But at the same time, every single person doesn't expect that [personal connection] of me either. They're just like 'Hey, can you just keep doing what you're doing?' because that in and of itself is helping."

COMMUNICATION AND MEDIATION

Figuring out who our neighbors are is only half the problem. The other half is communicating clearly with them.

Have you ever sent an email and received a reply that so misunderstood your intent that you just had to laugh? Or maybe, after a thirty-minute conversation with a spouse or close friend, you both realized you had been talking past each other the whole time? What about words you meant to comfort, but that came out clumsy and unkind, or lulls in your listeners' attention that led them to miss your caveats and hear only the declarations?

This kind of confusion between what you intend and what other people understand you to mean arises in large part because communication is mediated. We can't directly transmit our thoughts and hearts to others, so we communicate through media—writing and so forth—which often imperfectly carry our meaning. Even speech, our oldest channel of communicating, is a form of mediation. Our mediated communication obstructs our abilities to fully see and understand each other. We witness what we can on the outside, but only God knows everyone's true heart and sees the intent behind our actions (1 Sam. 16:7).

Though we usually spot obvious miscommunications, we often act as if our communication is direct or that any mediation is irrelevant, and then we make errors because we assume we completely understand another person's speech or behavior.[1] Mediation clouds something in the message, but we and our neighbors often can't quite grasp why we're having difficulties understanding each other. Sometimes those miscommunications are mundane ("Whoops, my joke didn't land"), but at other times something bigger is at stake. Our neighbors see only facets of us, never the whole picture of who we are, and what they see gets convoluted by the sometimes-wavy glass of communication.

I remember the time I told a friend how much I hated a class we were taking, and she was shocked, given what a class clown I was. But my laughter was me insisting the class not waste my time *and* be boring. Another time, some church members told me, "You were so sunny when you first started working here, we thought for sure it was an act, but now we've realized that's who you are." In my naivety, I didn't realize someone could see my enthusiasm and assume it was an act. These aren't only my stories. We have all had experiences where, in ways both significant and relatively inconsequential, we have been misunderstood because mediation obscured something true about who we are.

The complexities of mediation have always been with us, but our present age increases the difficulty. First, instead of being ourselves only in delimited neighborhoods, like our local congregation or our nonprofit's volunteer group, we communicate with more people, some of whom (perhaps many of whom) we don't personally know.

Second, it's more challenging because the messaging around many kinds of virtual media promises immediacy and hyperreality, but websites, podcasts, emails, and social media are as mediated as any other kind of communication. Most forms of physical media are obviously mediated, because of the gatekeeping involved in producing something and the time lapse between its creation and consumption. For example, the book you're reading has gone through the whole apparatus of professional publishing before getting into your hands. But virtual media, especially social media, often eliminate much of that gatekeeping, the editing and time for personal reflection on what is said, and the time between inception and publication. For instance, in a move that might feel completely transparent, I could jot down a social media post and immediately share it to the public, without even a second glance to make sure the punctuation was correct. Despite the differences, both the social media post and the book mediate my communication to you.

Third, we now have to consciously learn the norms of newer media. We have a lifetime's experience to rely on when communicating in person and have explicitly learned how to communicate through some kinds of media like sermons or essays. But with ever-proliferating forms of social media, we don't have that experience and training stored away to draw on intuitively when we are creating or using a given medium. So we have to learn its norms often practically from scratch. (Never mind that we're also learning how to use the technology, not just how to communicate with it.) In addition, the norms of newer media may change more quickly than with older forms, resulting in dramatically varying expectations from different people, and making it difficult to refine our use of them over the years.

Yet newer forms of media are fundamentally similar to older ones as they relate to being ourselves. Newer media, especially social media, merely highlight and increase the difficulty that was there before. Yes, there are apparent differences in the immediacy of some forms—think of the potential for celebrities and politicians to communicate swiftly and directly to their followers. But for our purpose of being fully ourselves in the ministry spotlight, the immediacy of some virtual media does not make them function differently from our older options. People can still see only some facets of us through our communication, never the whole picture.

DIFFERENT TOOLS FOR DIFFERENT CONVERSATIONS

How then can we communicate to different neighbors through our various options, from in-person media like sermons and songs, to physical media like books and magazines, and virtual media like websites, emails, and anything we post on a social platform? One way to approach this question is by thinking of these options as tools with which to love our neighbors and express ourselves. Sometimes we use a tool expertly. Sometimes we try one out and decide it isn't for us. Sometimes we make do with a tool because it's the tool we have and know how to use; it isn't perfect, but it will get the job done. Sometimes we see others' tools—whether the latest social-media platform or the venerable dinosaur we call a topical sermon—and react with a tinge of jealousy (Look at the shiny thing the kids are all using!) or with disdain (Why are they wasting their time with that?). Neither of those emotions helps us choose our tools wisely. What our colleague uses isn't necessarily suitable for our own setting. We don't have to use skillfully every tool in the hardware store, much less own them all. We simply need to use a few tools well.

When choosing which tools to use in ministry, especially in the context of being ourselves to more distant neighbors, we should first consider the range of nuance possible with a given format (think of a book versus a photograph's caption) and decide whether our message fits in that package. This is especially important when we think about what level of detail a given medium allows us as we show up as ourselves. Nonprofit leader Nikki Toyama-Szeto tells me her strategy when communicating primarily to strangers is to "show up authentically but also to show up simply, because to show up with a tremendous amount of complexity is to introduce a lot of room for misinterpretation." In these settings, Toyama-Szeto is still herself, "just more simple." Increasing simplicity tracks with an increasingly distant audience, whereas increasingly closer relationships allow for more and more nuance.

Youth leader Anita Smallin puts this concept into concrete terms: "I'm allowed to drink alcohol—this is not a problem. But I also minister to teenagers, so don't tag me in a picture with alcohol." In making this distinction, Smallin isn't hiding something about herself and her life, but wisely taking into account both the lack of nuance in a single picture and the context of her ministry to adolescents.

Second, we should consider whom we can reach through different media. Can we build new relationships? Strengthen existing ones? Communicate a similar message but from a different angle or context? Virtual media in particular have expanded the size of our neighborhoods. "Because of this medium called the Internet, we are able to basically preach to the public," says Sohn. "I write. People read. These are people who never will come to church, and that's fine, but my writing is still helping them spiritually." Instead of being discouraged that people aren't coming to church in person, she uses the tools she has to go to them.

Virtual media, especially social media, have also impacted how we find out information about the people we minister to and with, by expanding our abilities to read a room without actively interacting. Just as we can read body language in person, we can silently notice what church members say to each other through online platforms. These public forums give us a real-time feel for what our neighbors are thinking about, making them a helpful factor in our decisions about what to address. For instance, pastor Magrey deVega uses social media "to get a temperature reading on how much an event has captured our consciousness in the moment," which in turn helps him decide if he should address a current event during a church service.

Finally, we should consider if we can reach the same people using different formats. Describing the casual conversations he has after a church service, pastor Reginald Smith tells me, "I do my best preaching in the narthex. And I do it in the narthex because it gives an opportunity to go deeper with people who are not on guard at that time." The change in medium from sermon to conversation and the change in location influence how people expect to interact with him and thus influence their willingness to engage.

Virtual media in particular open new ways to connect with the people we already know, allowing us conversations spanning geography and vocation in a way that is nearly impossible to accomplish in person. For instance, while earning her doctorate in the United States, Riches maintained a lively dialogue with her home community in Australia: "They disagreed with me going to do a PhD as being ministry, as well as almost everything I posted, and the way in which I was writing it. They disliked the tone I used to have discussions. So I used Facebook as a way to continue the discussion and explain things more fully to them. I also allowed them to have a say into what was being taught, and then I began to understand why they disagreed with some of the things that were being said. That made me, I believe, a better scholar in the long run."

SAME PERSON, DIFFERENT TOOLS

While acknowledging the shifts we make across media and to different audiences, many people I interviewed point out that they are still integrated in who they are as they communicate: they are the same people, just using different tools. "If I'm not willing to share it during coffee hour talking to people or during prayer time, then I'm not going to share it online," says pastor Bruce Reyes-Chow. "I don't draw a distinction between online and in-person interaction and try not to encourage people to do that, because you have to be genuinely *you* in both spaces. That consistency is what I think gives us our authority and models for people not to fragment and compartmentalize life so much."

If we want to be integrated, we can't deliberately set ourselves up for *dis*integration, such as when we circumvent our neighborhoods by communicating anonymously or when we purposefully create multiple online accounts—one for polite announcements, one for the supposedly "real us" to vent. "What do you have to hide?" asks Smallin. "I can't play the game of having two accounts. I can't keep up with it, and it feels disingenuous to me." As with alter egos, the impulse to be anonymous or fragmented is often evoked by our being at odds with our environment, making it a warning signal that something needs to change.

Instead of disintegration, we can take into account the variety of media available to us. Then we can thoughtfully choose which registers to speak in or which facets of ourselves we make more prominent (a sermon calls on different areas than a personal essay), while still being the same person across our in-person, physical, and virtual means of communication. As Rozella Haydée White puts it, "I never want a person encountering me in one space, and another person encountering me in a different space, to talk about me, and I'm two different people to them."

For all the differences between kinds of media, Reyes-Chow, Smallin, and White are getting at the basic similarity in how we use media: we are still ourselves, being ourselves across the various ways we communicate. Our neighbors see different facets of us and have different ways of conversing with us, depending on which medium we use. But even if others cannot see us fully, we can still be integrated and wholly ourselves.

✳ ✳ ✳

KEY TAKEAWAYS

We are only ourselves in relationship with others, and we can be neighbors when we choose a relationship with anyone we encounter. The endless, unknowable audience of virtual media is an illusion.

Communication is mediated, and only God sees everyone's true intent. Misunderstandings arise when we mistakenly think we fully understand another person when the mediation has obscured something.

Mediation is more complex today than in the past because we communicate with a wider range of people. We often use media that seem to eliminate mediation between creator and audience, and we have to learn the norms of newer media.

Different kinds of media bring out different facets in ourselves and allow for different types of conversation with our neighbors.

DISCUSSION QUESTIONS

1. A neighbor is "one who chooses a relationship with anyone they encounter." How does this definition of "neighbor" resonate with you?
2. When have you felt as if you were speaking to an unknown audience?
3. What is a misunderstanding you've experienced due to mediation?
4. How do you think virtual media are similar to and different from other media?

5. What are some kinds of media you use, and which neighbors are you intending to speak to? What is your relationship to them?
6. Given the flattening effect of some media, how can you be "more simple" in your self-presentation?
7. Have you experienced an impulse to be anonymous or fragmented in how you communicate to different people? If so, how were you able to remain integrated?

Chapter 5
SKEWED REALITY OR A SLICE OF LIFE?

Some pleasant evening, look at the waxing or waning moon—the sliver of crescent popping against the darkening sky, perhaps with the moon's entire night side faintly visible as earthshine illuminates craters and mountains on its surface. This limited view, where we see only a distant slice of what we know is a three-dimensional sphere, resembles others' perspectives on our lives: 100-percent real, while being a small fraction of the whole. This chapter examines that bright crescent—the part of us that is publicly visible—and how we can decide what it should include. Even though it's not always a straightforward process, we must intentionally choose our ways of being in public; if we don't, we will jeopardize our privacy (and potentially that of our family members) and scatter our limited energies instead of channeling them.

Before we can even think about what aspects of ourselves to put in the "slice of life" that we share publicly, we must consider the possible effects of our actions. That pause to deliberate can feel manipulative or calculating, as if the impulse to craft, curate, or edit is itself disingenuous, as if we're trying to get away with something or fool the people around us into thinking things are better than they are. If our actions don't seamlessly align with our immediate gut feelings (as with *authenticity as naturalness*), then we may feel as if we are acting fake and thus less ourselves.

But the pause to weigh our possible actions and their likely consequences gives us time to make wise choices. Wisdom includes discerning what to share publicly about ourselves and what to reserve for the people closest to us. Being private isn't the same as being secretive or hiding our light under a bushel basket. Instead, it shows that we understand how to be ourselves in public settings and that we have appropriate places to be more vulnerable. Our intent can change forethought from wisdom to manipulation. Only we ourselves, in relationship with God and with wise counsel, can know our motivations.

That icky feeling of fakeness is there for good reason though. It reminds us of the ever-present possibility of distorting the truth. That gut feeling warns us against hypocrisy and bullshit; it alerts us to our human tendency to skew reality. I'm probably not the only one who has watched someone publicly gush about their spouse, even though everyone close to them knew their relationship was foundering. In cases like this, the issue isn't giving forethought to what people see through the window into our lives, but the fake props on display. Deciding to keep something private—even something as important to our identity as our marriage and problems there—is quite different from bluffing a better, fancier, holier life (and, with wise consideration, there are appropriate times to share our struggles, as chapter 7 discusses in more detail).

There is no inherent dishonesty in revealing only some of our whole selves in public. When we realize this, it's easier to understand how healthy this "slice of life" approach can be. "I don't have to put everything out there in order to be known or loved or understood," says writer Cara Meredith. Speaking of her memoir, she holds her index finger and thumb an inch apart, then stretches her

arms wide: "I shared *this* much of a story that was and is
so big." But the honesty of that slice connects with people.
"A lot of the feedback I've gotten, especially from men, is,
'Wow, you were really vulnerable.' And I'm like, actually I
wasn't, I just went deep on that one percent of the story."
We too can share a slice of our life, one that goes deep and
remains connected with the rest of our lives, even if our
neighbors can't see the rest. With pastor Lydia Sohn we
can say, "Here's one piece of my life that I'm sharing with
the world," and feel comfortable in that honest slice.

THE ILLUSION OF PROXIMITY

As positive as this slice-of-life approach is, many of our
neighbors assume they can see our whole lives. In previous
chapters, we have alluded to how some people think they
know us better than they do. One reason for this misperception comes from an illusion of proximity. Sometimes people
encounter many aspects of our lives without being relation-
ally close to us, a situation that convinces them they are closer
to us than they really are. (It's similar to how someone could
know a lot about the Bible without knowing God very well.)

While this misperception could happen in the past,
our use of virtual technologies like social media multiplies the
potential for it, by revealing parts of us that previously were
out of sight to the public. We don't necessarily have closer
relationships with our more distant neighbors, but they can
see more of our lives than before. Previously, only people
close enough to us to be in our office would have come across
the formal family photos on our desk—not exactly a private
space, but not one open to total strangers. Today though,
we can make our candid family photos completely public,

and instead of people hearing us only on Sunday mornings speaking from the pulpit, we chat on a podcast they hear in their cars, homes, or directly in their ears.

With social media in particular, some people mistakenly imagine their limited sightline into our lives is complete, behind-the-scenes access, rather than more akin to the edited content of a magazine or a family's Christmas newsletter. As a result, they may see what we share as representative of the whole, forgetting that the public slice of our whole selves more often highlights our good hair days and special occasion meals, not the saltines and peanut butter scarfed over the kitchen sink. Unfortunately, they may see us through the flattening effects of social media and believe that we are as one-sided in person as we seem on social media. They may feel betrayed when they find out things about us that they hadn't known. They may imagine we cannot understand them and their messy lives if our lives seem perfect. If they do eventually encounter our own mess, they may think we have been hypocritical because they couldn't see it before.

Much of the illusion comes from mistaking informality for a close relationship—an easy conflation to make, since closer relationships typically bring more informality. During the COVID-19 pandemic, I saw others' living rooms, offices, and basements, and they saw mine during our virtual meetings. Even with backdrops of perfectly coordinated art, bookshelves, and houseplants, we knew ring lights, comfy pants, and tangled computer cords were just offscreen. Lighthearted informality was always one cat's tail away, even if Mr. Whiskers lay low on a given call.

This window into the privacy of our homes could sometimes feel like intimacy. After all, we entered people's homes and met their pets for the first time, often in rooms we wouldn't usually encounter in a more formal event like a dinner party. We saw markers of closeness—someone's kitchen, someone's bedroom, someone's kid hamming it up for the audience or nonchalantly throwing up (true story). But what we experienced was informality, not relational intimacy.

Here's a way to think about the difference: Imagine two workplaces, one with a dress code of polos and khakis, and another where suits are the norm. Do you automatically know one set of coworkers better in the first place than in the other? Not at all. The relative informality of the setting doesn't correlate with, much less cause, depth and vulnerability in those relationships.

So too with the informality in much of our virtual world. Casualness prompts us to feel as if we're closer to each other than we are, leading us to misread the proximity as intimacy. If the people we serve have this misperception, they may not notice uneven power dynamics or our professional boundaries. They may also misread our friendliness as a deeper, more vulnerable friendship.

DECIDING WHAT SLICES TO SHARE

Given the potential for people to mistake the slice of our life for the whole, and our own potential to skew that slice, how should we decide what to share publicly? Sometimes there's a simple answer to the question of what's relevant to the people we are talking with, but often the answer is more complex, and we must take into account our personal needs and preferences. (Later chapters consider how to respond to the needs of others.)

Our needs are especially for privacy and for limiting the energy we use in one area of our life so that we have reserves for other areas. Privacy and energy are not one-size-fits-all categories, so the rest of this chapter explores *how* to establish your own boundaries (not *what* they specifically should be), with the goal of protecting you from unwanted publicity and burnout. Finally, this chapter circles back to the question of telling the truth with the public slice we share, rather than a slanted version of it, while later chapters continue with other angles on this question, including areas of controversy, difficult circumstances, and corporate worship.

Protecting Our Privacy

No bright line splits our life into public and private categories, and what is private to one person is public to another. Regardless of what specifics are public or private, we *can* be private people in public-facing ministry, and we ourselves are responsible for determining our personal boundaries.

Let's use our families to think about the issue. Some people rarely mention their family members. Others talk about their family publicly by centering themselves in whatever they share; their stories focus on their own experiences and give relative privacy to their family members, even if the narratives peripherally include them. For still others, being themselves in public includes telling their familial stories. Professor Eunjoo Mary Kim, for instance, tells me that "transparency is important to show who I am and what I teach. So I am very honest. I like to share my family story with students, and even in teaching or preaching . . . I don't see a difference or dichotomy between my personal life and my career."

In each perspective, the important thing isn't *what* is private to us, but *why* it is private. For many people, their answer comes down to personal preference and the preferences of their family members, which they discern through an ongoing dialogue. "Because of my social-media presence, people would be surprised to learn that I used to be a very private person, and to this day, my husband remains a very private person," says professor Karen Swallow Prior as she describes her transition into a public role. "So we've had to do a lot of negotiating about what I share on social media." Similarly, pastor Philip DeVaul makes collaborative decisions with his family, a practice he traces to his baptismal covenant: "We vow before baptism that we will seek and serve Christ in all people, love our neighbors as ourselves, and that we will respect the dignity of every human being. Respecting the dignity of every human being means respecting, in my case, my wife's dignity and my children's dignity. And part of their dignity is that they get to decide how they're represented out in the world and on social media."

Because of these conversations, Prior and DeVaul can share what they and their families are comfortable with sharing. We can use a similar process when we are deciding what is private or public about ourselves as individuals, such as when we bring our closer friends into conversation about this decision to gain their perspective and discern where our boundaries are. Choosing not to share facets of ourselves out of a concern for privacy is different from not sharing because we are ashamed of ourselves or afraid of others' responses, and these conversations can help us discern if our seeming impulse toward privacy is disguising shame or fear.

Protecting Our Energy

We might not want to share some areas, not because they are private, but because of the energy it takes to share them.

Since our energy is limited, sometimes we choose not to share something so that we can conserve energy for other aspects of our lives. No one person can do it all, and we have to be wise in spending our finite energies, because when we say yes in one area, we must say no to others. This opportunity cost is the first factor we should consider when deciding *what* amount to energy to spend *where*.

For instance, as a prolific musician, professor, and preacher, Braxton Shelley finds that extensive social-media commentary is often not worth the time it takes to produce, since his sermons, seminars, and academic writing take precedence. Plus, he risks spending time preaching to the choir. Most people who follow him online have similar viewpoints on controversial issues, so why put his energy there, when he could focus on prophetic preaching? It's not that Shelley isn't speaking up. Rather, he consciously chooses to speak up where he believes his voice matters most.

Second, we need to consider what medium we are using, since what we implicitly promise in terms of relational energy often varies with the medium we use. For example, imagine that a church member asks you a theological question over lunch. It's complicated, but you still give your answer your best effort. Now imagine the same question coming to you via email. You wouldn't ignore an in-person question, but for the same complicated, nonurgent question via email, you might wait a few days to respond. Why the difference in response time? Depending on your perspective, you might chalk it up to poor time management or possibly to excellent time management. But as I see it, the difference is primarily about the reasonable expectations of engagement for a given medium.

Social media platforms in particular can be tricky to navigate because they open us up to ongoing engagement with responses—all of which means using our energy. (Think of starting an unmoderated conversation as planting a garden and then forgetting it. It would be better to have left the ground wild than to create a mess of cross-populating watermelon and zucchini.) As a pastor who actively engages with parishioners through social media, DeVaul tells me that when he decides whether to post something potentially controversial, "I will only say something if I feel like I'm willing to stay in the conversation to be present, and argue, and listen, and be wrong." That doesn't mean every person gets the same depth of response or that he doesn't moderate these conversations, but that he posts expecting to engage, and posts only if he feels ready and able to engage. "When I speak politically, I try to speak in a way that is, I hope, reflective of where Jesus is, but I also require myself to leave myself open for critique."

Third, we should consider our environment and relationships. As explored in chapter 1, relationships and work environments that are nourishing give us energy instead of depleting it, whereas the opposite is true when those factors confine us. Being ourselves takes more energy when we don't fit our role's archetype, when other people misunderstand who we are, and when our fullness of self isn't wanted on a fundamental level. "I have to protect certain parts of me from certain people," explains professor Lakisha Lockhart in describing how her self-presentation varies with different people. "A lot of times the world tries to fragment us and tell us that we're inauthentic," she observes, "but we're just protecting ourselves and our energy."

A large factor tied to energy is what we risk in sharing ourselves. Professor and activist Leah D. Schade, for instance, tells me about a time when she had to limit her activism because of the threats people made to her and her family. Our relative risk depends on who we are, our environments, and other factors, many of which relate to our relative privilege. "What's at risk for people is huge," Lockhart points out when I ask her about speaking up about controversial issues. "What's at risk for a woman of color to be behind a pulpit and say a certain thing versus a white man to be behind a pulpit—it's a risk, and some people have a bigger risk than others." When deciding if and when to speak up, we should take into account our relative privilege, as discussed earlier in relationship with our relative powers to influence others.

Sometimes when dealing with something controversial, we can lessen our energy expenditure by drawing on others' work and words instead of using our own. For instance, we can float an idea by sharing an article with someone to ask what they think. Instead of arguing for or against a specific point, or committing to a long-term conversation, we start with the implicit argument that we can talk about the topic and use another's words to begin. Sandhya Jha, an ordained minister active in justice work, describes her itinerant preaching as this kind of springboard for conversations, telling me, "I'm a ringer for folks who can't talk about a lot of stuff. [The pastor] can have me come in, and then they're like, 'That was interesting. I wouldn't have put it that way, but I think I might agree with her. What do you all think?'"

In the end, the fact that we give our energies through public ministry shouldn't necessarily deter us from sharing. On the contrary, it is often a wise way to expend energy. If we realize we spend comparatively less energy than our colleagues, due to factors like environment and privilege, that knowledge may prompt us to devote more energy than we otherwise might. What matters is using that limited energy with discernment and love.

BULLSHITTING, BRAGGING,
AND SELF-CENTEREDNESS

Let's go back to where this chapter started. While sharing a slice of our life isn't fundamentally dishonest, we can skew that slice by obscuring our flaws and difficulties. We can lean so much into specific facets of our lives that we misrepresent who we are and how our lives are going on the whole. We can lie by omission just as much as we can lie by commission. And, frankly, we can be self-centered.

Sometimes our behavior isn't lying so much as bullshit. Lying, by nature, is always tethered to truth, but bullshit, "which involves making assertions without paying attention to anything except what it suits one to say," according to philosopher Harry G. Frankfurt, "is a greater enemy of the truth than lies are," because it is fundamentally disconnected from truth.[1] Frankfurt observes that "the fact about himself that the bullshitter hides . . . is that the truth-values of his statements are of no central interest to him."[2] As Frankfurt notes, "telling lies does not tend to unfit a person for telling the truth in the same way that bullshitting tends to do. Through excessive indulgence in the latter activity, . . . a person's normal habit of attending to the ways things are may become attenuated or lost."[3] In our attempts to present a shiny life to others, we may become unconcerned with telling the truth about ourselves, and so fall into a worse error than self-deception or intentionally lying to others.

With that in mind, let's consider how both sharing good news and speaking about our faith practices (an important way to normalize Christian behaviors) bring the potential for bullshitting, bragging about our righteousness, and being self-centered.

We've probably all seen similar scenarios: We've watched people proclaim their happiness and wondered, "Doth he protest too much?" We've known people in one context and been taken aback at their behavior in another setting—not because the setting was that different, but because their actions in different contexts were at odds with each other. We've seen people—including ourselves—use personal authenticity as an excuse to be self-centered.

It isn't easy to spot our heart's impulse toward bullshitting, bragging, or self-centeredness, because our actions can look good while our motivations are wrong. On one hand, sharing our devotional practices, our ways of raising our children, or our volunteer and activist work can all be valid forms of being a role model. On the other, they may be a decoy to take eyes away from our lives' blemishes, or they may be performative good works—a modern-day version of the trumpet announcing our almsgiving (a.k.a. tooting our own horn) as we try to latch on to whatever issue is trending to make ourselves look good. "How can I be more woke than you? How can I be more affected than you?" an activist and professor named Brandy asks rhetorically about this kind of performance. The potential for doing good just to be seen by others is ever present.

Discerning Our Motivations

Since we can't control how others perceive our good news or our attempts to model Christian behaviors, how can we share this good in our lives without disconnecting that slice from the whole picture—the picture that we know includes good and bad, but that our neighbors can't fully appreciate? How do we gauge our motivations, especially tendencies toward self-centeredness, given how easily we camouflage them, even to ourselves? New Testament scholar Craig C. Hill points out that "it is a tricky business, both because of the human tendency to self-deception and because of the differing perceptions and motives of others. An arrogant word may be veiled with innocence, and an innocent word may be judged as arrogance."[4]

I'm reminded of the difference in Christians' reactions to difficult musical pieces when they're played in worship services. In some traditions, a musician is likely to be criticized for showing off by selecting a flashy piece. In other traditions, the same musician and pieces would be interpreted as a testament to God's marvelous gift of music—how wonderful that God gives musicians their abilities to write this music and their aptitude to realize it in sound! Strikingly, neither interpretation has to do with the musician's own heart. Showing off is only about motivation, not others' perceptions, but we often think we can recognize showing off in others. Perhaps we do, and perhaps we don't; it's the intentions that matter.

Let's think about this through the lens of self-centeredness. Self-centeredness is a way to compensate for an insecurity in who we are. When we do not feel worthy, we grab at whatever makes us feel better than others and highlight those things to make up for our inner belief that we aren't good enough. In contrast, being more fully ourselves is about being more and more in the image of Christ. The closer we are to God, the more truly we are ourselves; so being ourselves cannot be self-centered or an excuse for egotism. Far from it! Believing in our worth as children of God is in opposition to these faults. "By being oneself authentically and superbly, we give God glory," observes Shelley. "When we call people brilliant, I think we're seeing that there's something in them that's also out of them.

In my tradition, we call that anointing, but whatever we call it, it is a way a human can point to God, not by talking about God, but by doing whatever one does."

Nonetheless, focusing on being more fully yourself can sometimes be an excuse for self-centered behavior. Let's look at ambition and status-seeking as a way to get at this distinction between being ourselves and being self-centered. In his study of ambition and status in the New Testament, Hill argues that ambition carries the potential for both good and bad, depending on what a person is ambitious for. In contrast, status-seeking is antithetical to Christianity, because it is about making ourselves better than our neighbors. Like egotism, status-seeking comes from the false belief that we aren't worthy in our current state, and it encourages us to puff ourselves up so we gain a higher social position.

Hill points out that ministry leaders "are in an especially conflicted position" because of how ambition powers our journey through our training and motivates our ministry: "I cannot imagine a fruitful pastor who is not ambitious, who does not dream dreams, see visions, and then work vigorously toward their realization. God is not laissez-faire, and faithful ministry is active ministry."[5] But because ambition is such close kin to status-seeking, we must be vigilant. "To be or not to be ambitious is thus not the question," writes Hill. "Instead, we must ask, 'Toward what are we ambitious and why?' The answer may well be elusive. It takes discernment of the sort most likely gained in the company of others who know us well and are permitted to speak to us truthfully. It is also won through searching and open prayer. We might fool ourselves, but we do not fool God."[6] So too with striving to be more fully ourselves. God knows our hearts and our sense of self-worth as God's children.

Given the starting point in understanding our motivations, we can continue to discern what to share in that public slice of our lives through the input of friends and mentors who inform our decisions. These people help us gauge how we present ourselves in these public spaces—if the slice of life we are sharing feels true, if we are making a holier-than-thou performance, if our tone of voice sounds like us or a what-a-preacher-sounds-like persona. Our closest friends, the ones who see just about the whole picture, should never see the slice we share and think it's make-believe. They can help us find the slice to share in honesty, humility, and care for our neighbors as well as ourselves.

TELLING THE WHOLE TRUTH IN HUMILITY

In conclusion, let's consider one slice of life that sometimes comes across as bragging: telling the truth about our accomplishments. Some people practically never publicly share news of their accomplishments because they don't want to brag. But while narrowing or omitting this kind of truth about ourselves may look like humility, it is not. "Me not sharing something incredible in my life—it's not really humble. It's just me not sharing," says writer Rozella Haydée White. Humility, she argues, is "not about playing small, as much as it is about always pointing back to the one who has given you the gifts, or made the way, or imparted the knowledge on you."

To conceptualize humility, she points to the practice of testifying. We should think about "sharing our successes as a testimony to who God is and what God has done—and I'm not talking about material things: I'm talking about the wisdom that we get, the doors that open, and the healing that happens. When we can share that, then I think we invite other people, not only to have a language around that, but to be on the lookout for how God works in their life."

One way to share in humility is by decentering ourselves, especially if we're sharing news that might encourage praise from people we have relational power over. Bragging points to ourselves as the source of goodness instead of God, and much of our intent to brag comes from a narrative's focus on us. Pastor Magrey deVega explains, "My default position is that if I'm going to talk about something good that's happened to me, I'm just going to let that be the intro into some deeper kind of spiritual truth that isn't about me." For instance, announcing his wife's pregnancy could have led to applause in a church service, so he says, "I just rolled right through the announcement and then went right into the heart of the spiritual truth I was trying to unpack." He's also used this strategy when sharing news that could more directly lead to perceptions of bragging, such as announcing a book publication.

It also doesn't hurt to occasionally point out publicly the reality that our lives are much bigger than the slice we typically share. The bedhead is not more real than the good hair day, but "keeping it real" can give a sense of sharing a more well-rounded perspective on our lives. By sharing some of that fuller picture, we can help more naive neighbors understand that no one's life is a glossy magazine spread.

Sharing ourselves without pride or shame often comes down to telling the plain old truth, while pointing to the source of that truth. Is it true God called you to be a youth leader? Is it true you can preach a soaring sermon? Did you win this or that award? Are you gifted to minister at deathbeds? There is no bragging in those facts. There's no bragging in admitting to the hard work and dedication it took to finish seminary, lead the youth seminar, or learn to sing those high notes. (There are no extra special brownie points for them either. You aren't closer to God because of those facts or despite them.) Instead of a false smallness or being opaque about ourselves and what we've created, we can—and should—use our public slice of life to spotlight God's handiwork in our lives.

✳ ✳ ✳

KEY TAKEAWAYS

Intentionally curating our public presentation is important and good, but it can feel disingenuous, partially because curation can be skewed, whether deliberately or not. We can share a "slice of life" in public ministry that is honest, deeply connected with our whole selves, and rooted in wisdom, even though the rest of our lives isn't publicly visible.

The illusion of proximity means some neighbors think they are closer to us than they are, possibly leading to their feeling confused and even betrayed when they realize our lives are bigger than the slice they can see, and to their assuming we have a more vulnerable relationship with them than we actually do.

In deciding what is private and public for us, the point isn't what we choose, but how and why we make our decisions. We may decide to keep parts of ourselves out of public ministry to protect our energy and prevent burnout.

Sharing good news can easily turn into bullshitting, bragging, and being self-centered, but we should still strive to tell the whole truth, while pointing to God.

DISCUSSION QUESTIONS

1. Have you felt deceptive—or actually been deceptive—by intentionally curating your public self?
2. What slice of your life do you want to share in your public ministry, and what aspects do you want to keep private?
3. Have you experienced informality being mistaken for a close relationship?
4. When you need to conserve energy, what aspects of yourself do you need to protect first?
5. When might striving to be yourself become self-centered?
6. What other strategies can you imagine to avoid bragging without concealing good news?

Chapter 6
FOR THE SAKE
OF OUR NEIGHBORS

Our decision to bring something into the public slice of our lives isn't determined solely by our needs and wishes. We are also called to be "all things to all people" (1 Cor. 9:22) and even to self-empty ourselves (Phil. 2:7). "Part of what's so hard about the job of the minister," explains educator Casey Stanton, "is that it isn't primarily about you and your needs: it's about you meeting people where they are."

Ministry demands boundaries and responsibilities for the sake of our neighbors, not to the exclusion of our own needs or in competition with them, but in concert together. Following the call to be "all things to all people" doesn't mean shape-shifting into whatever form we think will please others or erasing ourselves completely. This call is not an invitation to chameleon-like ministry but a call to speak the Gospel so that different people can hear it—to consider how others may understand differently than we do, and to learn to speak in their dialects so that they can better hear the Good News. We can't minister as someone else, only as our own selves, but we can learn to share the Gospel in different ways.

This chapter begins with the bigger picture of how others' needs impact what we share—both the valid ways this can happen and the times those effects become problematic—and how integrity undergirds our decision-making process on what to put into the public eye. Then it explores how our neighbors can shape how we speak about our faith and about controversial issues.

Knowing that the following chapters also consider how others' needs continually inform our public ministry, let's take a snapshot of our public slice of life from the perspective of how our neighbors shape it. First, we may limit how much of ourselves we reveal in a given setting. Paul Vasile describes his approach to leading ecumenical worship, often with people he doesn't know well, asking himself, "How much do these folks really need to know about me for us to do the work we need to do right now?" and finding a productive constraint: "Sometimes I will find myself subverting my need to self-disclose for the greater good of the work, in what I hope is a good way." This focus on others comes out of love. He explains, "My work has often been to help remind myself and the groups of people I'm working with of their humanity and of that shared experience of what it means to be human. I'm not saying the particulars aren't important, but I try to fundamentally offer in the work I'm doing a shared sense of, 'I'm like you: I'm a human being.'"

Second, we may carefully select what we say in public, holding it up to the critical eye of others' potential misinterpretations and criticisms. Professor Karen Swallow Prior describes gaining a wider public audience for her writing, one that she didn't ask for and that can be vitriolic to her as a woman in some conservative circles. In the past, her public audience was her students—people with whom she could build a relationship during conversations over a semester or more, people who weren't observers but cocreators of the environment in which each conversation took place. "There have been some growing pains and bumps along the way for me to realize that other people don't have the context," she tells me. "They don't know me, and they're just seeing a tweet out of context. So I have to be more careful because I do have a wider audience. I'm constantly negotiating: Am I censoring myself by not sharing this thing I think is really funny? Or am I being responsible to my wider audience?"

As with Vasile, these limitations result from love. Prior explains, "I really go through a lot of thinking about my integrity and authenticity as I try to be myself to this audience that I didn't really ask for, and that I might not really like, but that I want to love: I need to figure out how to love them in the way that I can."

Third, we may joyfully step back to make room for others' growth. It's not that our voice doesn't matter or that our opinions aren't valid, but that our moment of silence allows another person to speak up. Writer Nicole Roccas explains, "I find it easy to share things that others may consider 'personal information.' And so for me, the question is often not, 'How can I be more vulnerable while still being authentic or maintaining professional distance?' It's often, 'How do I self-select the ways I am willing to be vulnerable? How do I pull back a little bit and create space?' You're trying to open up space where others can connect with you, so you don't want to put so much of yourself out there that others have no space left to put themselves out there and seek connection."

Usually we think about the positive effects of our enthusiasm and ideas, but many of us can fall into the pitfall of overfunctioning, by doing for others what they should do for themselves. Our brightness, hard work, ambition, creativity—while all good—can unintentionally limit others. Sure, a grownup can do the science project better than the eight-year-old, but that defeats the project's purpose. Similarly, in many congregational and nonprofit settings, often the point isn't that we do the work the supposedly "best" way, but that we facilitate the ministry that volunteers are responsible for.

WHAT BOUNDARIES AND
RESPONSIBILITIES ARE NOT

We can't talk about our responsibilities to others and how those responsibilities influence what we do without pointing out how some of us are far more likely to unduly suppress ourselves than to overfunction or otherwise limit our neighbors—so much so that I hesitate writing any encouragement to factor others' needs into our decisions about our public slice of life, except in the most obviously Christian ways. The people who most need a warning are least likely to heed it, and the people who are least likely to overfunction are the most likely to think I'm admonishing them. Professor Lakisha Lockhart recounts a mentor's advice that "you don't have to lower your light or dim who God has created you to be and the things that God has gifted you with, just to make other people not feel intimidated. Because if they feel intimidated, that's their work to work on." It's true: other people's choices are *their* choices, and we have to discern with our trusted counselors what our appropriate boundaries and responsibilities are.

So let's think about the limits Vasile, Prior, and Roccas describe, and what makes those limits positive. Their self-emptying is a far cry from the smallness that derives from shame—the bushel basket of all bushel baskets hiding our God-given light—or that results from an environment squashing us down. Maria McDowell describes the difference in her own life. She was initially in a religious space where she had to actively limit herself—including ignoring her call to ordained ministry—to remain there. But now, as a pastor, she experiences a radically different kind of boundary, one she chooses to better serve her congregation. She explains, "It is a real joy and a blessing to sometimes have to make myself small for another person if it will help them. I'm not doing it because of their fear or unwillingness to change or to listen to something different. I'm doing it out of love for them because it will help them in this moment."

Accepting boundaries is not about getting people to like us or about contorting ourselves; being "all things to all people" doesn't mean we should rummage through a grab bag of personas for whichever one we think someone might prefer. There is a fundamental difference between the mind-set that says, "I choose to put others' needs before my own because I am able to do that in a healthy way," and the mind-set that says, "I put others' needs before my own because my needs do not matter." A person with the most robust personal integrity is also the person who can most empathetically serve others for the long term without burning out. Pastor and writer Lydia Sohn describes this realization in her life: "My thinking was that in order to be a good pastor, I just had to make everybody happy and do what they wanted me to do. And then I quickly realized—thank the Lord!—that if I did that, it would burn me out, and it wouldn't actually make me a good pastor at all, because I wouldn't be fulfilled or full of life."

As with much of the conversation about being more fully ourselves, thinking about how we share ourselves in ministry comes down to love for our neighbors. When we hunch over because we don't believe we are worthy to be ourselves or because our environment doesn't give us the room to stand tall, we aren't operating out of love. But when we know who we are, we are freed up to focus on others and, in so doing, to give God glory. By learning how to live as ourselves in the world, we can more intentionally choose to prioritize others' needs without acting as doormats or enablers.

CONTROVERSIAL ISSUES

With boundaries and responsibilities in mind, let's consider how others' needs influence our faith language and the ways we speak up on controversial issues, beginning with the latter. Both areas are ripe for misunderstandings. Both connect to our responsibilities as representatives of faith. Both spring from our hearts. We speak up about the controversial issues we care about, and our ways of speaking to and about God go deep, often back to our cradle.

A point of clarification: when I say "controversial issues" here and throughout this book, I mean areas that are genuinely up for debate in our particular circles. For example, in some circles, Christians drinking alcohol is a controversial issue, whereas in many others it is a nonissue, either because "of course they can" or because "of course they can't." What I do not mean by "controversial issues" is issues that are controversial in other circles of Christianity or the public sphere, but not in our given setting.

Let's set the stage for our responsibilities in these areas. We minister to people who are not exactly like us. We work in the "big tents" of politically and socially diverse congregations and denominations—what Leah D. Schade, in her research on fostering meaningful congregational dialogue on controversial issues, calls the "purple zone."[1] Even groups that are more politically, theologically, or socially homogeneous don't agree on every single topic, every single time. Beyond our local setting, some of us minister in pandenominational or nonreligious settings where we reach people with considerably different customs for talking to and about God.

As a result, we have to discover how to be ourselves amid the constraints of controversy and of communicating outside our usual modes of expression. With Andrew Davis, we need to ask a fundamental question: "What does integrity in a system like this look like?" As an Orthodox priest in the United States, Davis not only deals with differences between dioceses, but ministers to a wide range of ethnic groups who, though all Eastern Orthodox, hold varying traditions accrued over centuries in their countries of origin, a problem that is compounded by some congregants mistakenly assuming that these customs and various bishops' directives are consistent across the denomination as a whole.

Truly, what *does* integrity look like in such a big tent?

When we think about our faith language and controversial issues, we have to begin with that desire for integrity in our lives. Our public slice of life must always be true to our faith and our whole selves.

Discerning Which Topics to Address

Thinking back to the metaphor of the crescent moon, we may imagine the brightest part as the loudest, which, for many of us, includes how we speak up on controversial issues. This aspect of ministry gets public attention, expresses our values, and fulfills our vocational responsibilities. Our calling is often what motivates us to speak up about controversial issues, and when we don't speak up about something that we feel called to address, we obscure something fundamental about us and our beliefs. As Molly Baskette points out to her congregation in the middle of difficult conversations, "I'm doing my best to interpret the Gospel and listen carefully to what God is saying to me and to the church, and I have an obligation to tell you what that is. That's why you called me: you called me to lead you. You can disagree with me—and I'm not going to tell you to agree with me—but you can't use that disagreement to stifle me either."

Each of us has particular areas we feel more called to speak about than other areas, and many of the people I interviewed described wading into controversy because of their calling to do so. For instance, children's minister Laura Wilson focuses on issues related to children, because of her calling and because she hopes her professional credibility makes people more willing to listen to her on these topics. Schade, an ordained minister and professor, describes being "driven by my understanding of my call and my response to the commands of Jesus to care for the least of these, to advocate for those who cannot speak for themselves, to amplify the voices that are not at the table, to be in solidarity with those who are affected by decisions that are beyond them, but that directly affect them."

This call gets at the issue of integrity. How and when should we speak up, knowing we risk fanning the flames of anger instead of changing hearts or promoting useful dialogue? When we're talking about issues close to our faith, we can't just say anything we please. We are responsible to follow our calling to speak up, *and* we are responsible to consider how our speaking up affects others beyond simply persuading them of something. M.R., a priest, describes the tension: "There's always the danger of being so shy, even cowardly, to talk about things that need to be addressed. I also see how the real possibility of trying to talk about a contentious issue could contribute to further division rather than bringing people together."

Part of the difficulty is not in a specific topic itself but in the perception that disagreement disrespects or rejects people. Wilson, for example, struggles with her calling to "react to things that are happening in the world that are unjust and that are tragic," while worrying that "if I say what I really think, am I going to close doors that need to stay open?" Is speaking up about something politically divisive "going to make parents less likely to come talk to me when they need help with their kids?" Her worry is not unfounded, given the polarized world of politics, where being on the "other team" can make instant enemies. Sometimes by simply mentioning a topic, much less taking a position on it, we alienate people by seeming to judge them or exclude them from our community.

Another part of the difficulty is that what is controversial varies widely—what would be controversial in one Methodist church's newsletter would not necessarily be controversial for another Methodist church in the next town over. Sometimes we incite a divisive conversation without meaning to, because we aren't aware the issue is thorny. And beyond specific hot-button issues, other people have varied and competing expectations for what we should or should not say, based on what they believe about us and our roles as faith representatives. If we have a public platform of any size or simply a pulpit on Sunday mornings, or if we have privilege attached to our race, sex, gender, or other factors, some people expect us to speak up on civic events and current debates, while other people expect silence, or they want us to speak up only if we agree with them.

It may even be that we don't need to speak up at all. Even if we have opinions that we feel are important on a given topic, it may not fall into our field of expertise or spiritual obligation. Maybe your church is determining its musical styles for corporate worship (and you know how contentious potential changes in congregations are wont to be). If you're the children's pastor, with no particular leadership role in music and worship, do you have a moral responsibility to stick your oar in and muddy the waters— or, as Proverbs 26:17 would have it, reach out and grab the poor dog's ears? Probably not. In cases like this, we aren't cowards if we do not speak up publicly. We are wisely minding our own business.

Speaking Up to Change Minds

Tackling hot-button issues takes labor, so let's bring our responsibility to speak up into conversation with the previous chapter's focus on wisely using our energy. Sometimes we need to speak up against the tide of popular opinion to stake our viewpoint and explain why we have arrived at that view as Christians. But many of the people I interviewed want the possibility of concrete change to justify the time and energy they use when speaking up. In the end, they aren't using their energy for a wishy-washy feeling of inspiration; they are calling for action.

Of course, we often have little hope of changing peoples' minds, and we know that logic won't budge cranky toddlers or conspiracy theorists. Braxton Shelley, a professor and ordained minister, points out that "people like being who they are, even if who they are is toxic," an observation that leads him to think "it is supremely arrogant for ministers, for people, for family members—for us to think we're going to make somebody so uncomfortable with their life that they're going to change because we tell them to." This dynamic is one reason nonprofit leader Nikki Toyama-Szeto is mindful of Jesus' caution against casting pearls before swine "lest they trample them under their feet, and turn again and rend you" (Matt. 7:6 KJV). She carefully discerns when she decides to engage with people about controversial issues: "I'm very mindful of when I go really deep. Are there the seeds indicating that my taking this risk is actually going to be fruitful, or is this just an exercise of hitting my own forehead against the wall?"

So many of us choose to selectively speak up and selectively dialogue with people, sometimes finding a way to move the needle even a little, if not 180 degrees. For example, musician Dan Forrest asks of his political social media posts: "Does this have the potential to encourage certain people or challenge certain people enough to where it's worth it?" He also considers how closely related to Christianity the specific issue is, since he cares more about the intersection of politics and Christianity than more tangential issues.

Keeping our sights on this change-making goal can embolden and invigorate us because it points to the bigger picture—to the Gospel expressed in our actions. As the Lutherans say: "God's work. Our hands."[2]

Following the Holy Spirit's Leading

Amid this complicated web of factors, we must follow the Spirit's lead in what to say. Following the Holy Spirit is our spiritual obligation, even if that calling makes us or our neighbors uncomfortable and makes us want to gloss over complicated, unwanted truths. I'm preaching to myself here, because after spending almost all my life in the

American Midwest and Southeast, I find that "midwestern nice" and its southern equivalent run deep in me. For a long time I thought of this as an unequivocal good: it is good to be nice to people. But what I didn't realize is how niceness cheaply imitates goodness on the surface while leaving out its integral structure. Hedging around the truth injures us, and what begins in basic courtesy can lead to hypocrisy. But there is no point to leading worship, teaching students, or whatever specific task of public ministry God has called us to, if we aren't speaking truth.

"You're not trying to blow up your church, you're trying to tend to a flock, and you're trying to understand their needs, fears, hopes, and dreams. And you're trying to speak to them as truthfully as you can with what you know about God's hopes and dreams for us and what God grieves about for us." That's how Stanton, a Roman Catholic educator, describes ministering in a local church and denomination that is politically and culturally diverse. On one hand, she describes the big tent as a "gift," because of how it makes her "suspend judgment and meet people where they are." On the other hand, being a leader in that kind of environment means that "out of deeply loving people, sometimes we have hard words we have to give, and we have to risk being rejected and people thinking we're mean."

Baskette takes a similar perspective, "I try to send a message that I am a pastor to everybody in this church. You may disagree with me, but I am still your pastor. I will love you. I will listen to you. I will treat you with respect. And please believe that my desire is to be in calm, loving, connected relationship with every one of you. Not to polarize." No matter how we choose to speak up about controversy or faith, loving others means following the Holy Spirit's lead to tell the truth out of a heart of love.

FAITH LANGUAGE AND A PLURALITY
OF EXPRESSION

Our faith language is another area where others' needs impact how we are in public. To be "all things to all people" as we minister the Gospel, we must consider the form our communication takes and how it reaches different people. We can change our speech so others can understand us; we can say the same thing, but with different words. In this practice, we are not changing ourselves but how we communicate. We are not altering the Gospel but speaking the Gospel so others can hear it. We can, as Vasile puts it, use a "plurality of expression" to share the Gospel and even to share ourselves, because underneath the shifts in how we share the Gospel and how we share ourselves is an ever-present rock of truth.

In his leadership of ecumenical worship, Vasile says, "It's been really helpful for me to learn many, many, many ways to say exactly the same thing. Regardless of the community I'm part of, part of what I'm doing is discovering the language that best resonates with this particular group of people I'm working with—with the hope that they're going to come along with me on that journey, and they're going to respond to the language I'm offering. And if they're not, I can adjust. I can try something different. I can find a new metaphor."

Even within a single congregation, the range of demographics and individual experiences can mean one way of speaking faith doesn't work for everyone. For instance, pastor Paul Rock describes leading three services at one congregation, where each service shifts the delivery of the same thematic message. "It's all authentic," he tells me, "but there's a little bit of a different dialect" in each service.

Even though we've all used strategies like this to communicate more effectively—adjusting our vocabularies to accommodate the children we talk with or the adults who don't know our professional jargon—adjusting our *faith* language (and how we share ourselves by speaking our faith) can feel inauthentic to who we are and what we believe. Because speaking about and to God is close to our hearts, it's easy to adopt the concept of *authenticity as naturalness* as the most relevant value. But this kind of authenticity can be detrimental to ministering to others who do not share our faith language. Instead, the concept of *sincerity* is much more helpful, because it allows us to evaluate whether we are speaking the truth with good intent. In sincerity, we can speak our faith using whatever tools (i.e., whatever language) we have at hand because our foremost aim is telling the truth, not using the turns of phrase that flow easily for us.

Another reason for the difficulty is that the same faith words can mean different things to different people. ("You say you're a Christian, but is Jesus Christ your personal Lord and Savior?" or "I believe that God is the maker of heaven and earth.") Similar things can be called by different terminology. (Does your church call them "prayer requests," "prayer intentions," "joys and concerns," or something else?) Though we try to keep the content consistent, we may inadvertently trip up on the nuances of different Christians' ways of speaking their faith.

Let's think about shifts in our faith language through the lens of public prayer. Prayer is probably the most visceral example of speaking faith from our heart. After all, changing how we speak *about* God is one thing, but intentionally changing how we speak *to* God, the One with whom we are in relationship, can feel like another thing entirely. So if we cultivate different ways of leading public prayer in order to invite others to pray with us, we may feel as if we are misrepresenting ourselves, our personal beliefs, and our habits.

When we think about the different ways we already pray, we can better imagine how to lead collective prayer when we're in spaces outside our faith home. Each of us has various ways to talk to God—differences we experience in our daily lives and that already feel comfortable to us. For instance, I have at least four ways of praying: prewritten personal prayers, extemporaneous public prayers, fill-in-the-blank templates I invent with my children ("Thank you God for _____"), and variations on a "Lord have mercy" theme that punctuate my everyday life. All of these are truly my prayers from the heart, even though the styles differ. Whatever the style of address, God hears us and knows everything about us—our intents, our backgrounds—unlike the people we are inviting into collective prayer with us. So it's our fellow neighbors, not God, who need us to pray so that they can also pray with us.

Here's how Brian Hehn experienced different ways of leading public prayer. When he began ministering pan-denominationally as part of his job with a nonprofit, he noticed his language depended on where he was, such as when he used different ways of opening and closing his prayers. At first, the shifts made him wonder if he was "being disingenuous," but then he realized these variations allowed others to pray with him. For example, Hehn says he might open prayer with "Father God" if that is part of the faith language of the people he is worshiping with. Praying this way doesn't contradict his beliefs (he doesn't say, for instance, "Father God, you are male, and the only right way to name you is by saying Father"), and it's not how he would pray at home. But in certain settings, this opening invites others into prayer with him. "It's always about people," he explains. "While we do have to have our own personal convictions, and I do firmly believe in doing no harm and standing up for people who are marginalized, I don't have any problem with changing the language of my prayer if it's helpful for a group of people to enter into that prayer with me."

Rock used the metaphor of dialects to describe the different services at his church. Professor Jean Kidula similarly uses this metaphor to imagine how our expressions of faith can sound different while sharing the same truth. For her, it's more than just saying one thing in different ways. The differences among dialects, says Kidula, "tell us something about our differences. But at the same time, they tell us something about the diversity of who God is."[3] Recall from the introduction that by sharing our individuality with others, we let them see an aspect of God. By extension, when we see others in their fullness, we see more of God. Kidula makes a similar connection in how we speak about God. "How vast is the sum" of God's thoughts, she says, referencing Psalm 139:17. We can experience some of that greatness by experiencing how others speak their faith.

So then, as we learn to speak the Gospel in ways others can hear, we are not only ministering to them, but we are glimpsing more and more of God as we experience others and their ways of speaking faith. Yes, others' needs impact the public slice of our lives, giving us boundaries and responsibilities to grapple with. At the same time, responding in love to our neighbors expands who we are and enriches our experience of God.

KEY TAKEAWAYS

Intentionally accepting boundaries and responsibilities can be a loving act of self-emptying that brings the Gospel to others in ways that they can better hear. We love our neighbors by making space for them. To be "all things to all people," we don't need to shape-shift according to our neighbor's preferences, but we should speak and live the Gospel in ways that other people can hear.

Most professional Christians minister in the "big tents" of denominations and organizations that include a relatively wide range of political and social views. That means we have to figure out how to talk about controversial issues in productive ways.

Adjusting our faith language can feel inauthentic to who we are and what we believe, but when we minister to diverse people, we have to learn how to speak the Gospel in different ways.

DISCUSSION QUESTIONS

1. What interpretations of "all things to all people" have you heard? Which ones resonate with your exegetical traditions?
2. How have you experienced constraints due to shame or being in an environment that was too small?
3. What truths that aren't polite or nice do you feel called to speak? What issues do you not bring up because you don't think your perspective will change minds?

4. What is a time you experienced a productive disagreement, and what is a time when it worsened the controversy?
5. What risks and privileges do you bring to speaking up about controversial issues?
6. How do you tailor your faith language to particular settings?
7. What do you think about the metaphors of dialects and plurality of expression as ways to imagine shared faith? How have you deepened your relationship with God by learning others' ways of verbalizing their faith?

Chapter 7

SHARING OUR VALLEYS
WITH OTHERS (OR NOT)

We professional Christians are all quirky, complicated, and sometimes difficult people. We have odd bits, gross habits, shirts buttoned up askew. We get sick, break up, and live with the same predicaments as everyone else. We have dark nights, times when God seems far from us, times when we inch forward so entirely by faith, we might as well be walking on water. Sometimes we're so in the valley that speaking about it would bring us to our knees. Maybe our journey is taking us right out of our faith homes and into others, or out of faith entirely. We're waiting for the diagnosis. We're tired, weary in well-doing. Our marriage is splitting at the seams, and we don't know yet if we can or should sew it back together. Maybe we don't want to blow up our lives, but damn, if we don't dream of throwing in this professional Christian towel and finding a nice nine-to-five, whatever-happens-at-the-office-stays-at-the-office kind of job.

Adding to the mess is the question of how to walk through a valley with integrity while being appropriate in our public ministry. Maybe you, like me, have seen how other people minister through their valleys and admired their testimony, yet struggled to reconcile what they do with your own impulse toward privacy. Maybe you see yourself as a strong, stoic person and don't want to change or lose that identity. Maybe you hear sirens warning you not to slip into manipulative oversharing whenever you receive encouragement to "share the hard stuff."

During a difficult season, our guarded words may feel deceptive or insincere at best. Talking about these times as they unfold feels premature, like an unfair burden to put on our congregations, or like an invasion of our privacy. Even years later, we may keep hard experiences close to our hearts, unwilling to disclose them. Sometimes our lives may intertwine with others' lives in ways that we can't discuss. A family member's mental health crisis acutely affects our own lives, emotions, and spiritual practices, but we can't tell that story with any specificity. A church member's experience weighs on us, but we can't mention it, except perhaps to a spouse or confidential colleague. Even though we live in a tell-all culture, we don't have to tell all of our stories. Yet we still want to speak the truth.

Besides the dangers of processing in public or betraying confidences, sharing our valleys can lead to other problems. Our doubts can become part of our professional identity, and while some people may be willing to live in that tension indefinitely, most of us want to find solid ground, not acquire a professional identity of perpetually balancing on a tightrope. The confessional mode can glamorize (and sometimes monetize) our sin or become a strange cart-before-the-horse situation where our public confession is our first and only one. On the other hand, if we aren't publicly transparent about our flaws and difficult circumstances, there's the feeling that we are hiding something.

Finally, we are often on a pedestal in our communities. Some people we minister to don't want to hear that faith leaders have hard times just like everyone else. They want their role models squeaky clean, and they don't want to hear any dark plot twists in the narratives of our lives.

Given these problems and sometimes-competing priorities, how can we be fully ourselves when we're walking through the valley? This chapter explores how we can keep the public slice of our lives consistent with the whole, even when we can't reveal everything difficult that happens. And it shows how sharing our valleys can be not only appropriate but a powerful way to live out our faith with our wider circle.

THREE KINDS OF VALLEYS

This chapter addresses three kinds of valleys. First, difficult circumstances. Some are short-term, and some are crosses borne for years. Some of these are immediately public but involve private time to process, such as the death of a family member. Some are private for a long time or indefinitely. Some are temporarily private, such as when someone waits for a confirmed medical diagnosis before telling others about their illness.

Second, the struggle that is our imperfect selves. We may make our more superficial flaws into lighthearted points of connection with others but be tempted to whitewash our deeper wounds and failings. Although we sometimes have good reasons to keep our flaws out of the public eye, this chapter delves into why we might want to be more transparent and why our mistakes should not be completely secret, regardless of our public choices.

Third, seasons of transition, particularly ones where we find ourselves in environments where we aren't as neat a fit as we once were. Sometimes our transitions involve our personal integrity on a deeper level. Perhaps we've grown, but our environments haven't. Maybe our faith is evolving in ways that are incompatible with our current church. Maybe we haven't changed but have realized a longstanding issue. While many transitions aren't valleys, such as when we're in a confidential job search, looking at the transitions closer to our heart also gives us insight into how to be honest during more mundane transitions.

In all these areas, public knowledge of a valley is distinct from processing it in public. Even if the people around us know about the circumstance, failure, or transition, they aren't necessarily privy to how we are dealing with it—and often shouldn't be, if we are still negotiating it. For example, a parent's death is usually public essentially as soon as we ourselves know, but we may not be able to share our grief for many months to come. Our divorce may be public, but we may not be ready to share anything more than the factual statement of legal truth, and maybe we will never be ready.

WHY TO SHARE OUR VALLEYS

If we don't understand the power of sharing difficult times, we may decide to take an easier route by keeping the mistakes and dark days in the shadows. But sharing can connect us with our neighbors through the similar messiness of our lives, normalize conversations about difficult experiences, and offer a role model of vulnerability and resilience. Most importantly, as pastor Lydia Sohn points out, as ministry leaders, we are "able to interpret those struggles through a theological lens." By sharing our valleys, we can point to Christ and help our neighbors walk closer to God in their own journeys.

Building Connection

Sharing our valleys builds trust with our neighbors, because they know we understand at least some of what they've endured. Even "the common ordinariness of life," observes pastor Magrey deVega, is something our neighbors can recognize in themselves. This kind of sharing helps get us off the pedestal and builds more mutual relationships with the people we minister with and to.

Even though we know everyone has valleys, we can be unbalanced in our public presentation. By sharing ourselves more holistically, we alleviate the problems of unrelenting positivity and hypocrisy. Writer Nicole Roccas explains, "I hate the feeling that I'm preaching or writing out of one side of my mouth, and then going on to commit the same sins I have just been writing against." So she says that when she is writing against a particular failing, "I may share select examples from my own life of how I haven't measured up."

It may feel as if our problems are heavier than those of our neighbors, but we have more in common than we realize. Though not everyone's valleys look exactly like ours, there's a subset of our audience that has had similar experiences or will someday. "When I share my struggles," Roccas tells me, "I usually don't have the feeling of, 'Oh gosh, are they going to think differently of me?' because I just assume that they know exactly what I'm talking about. So I have very little shame in sharing my struggles—and those struggles include deep doubts, times of profound loss, a sense of meaninglessness, all of that. I just assume that most people have gone through times like that."

Sometimes we're even in the valley with our neighbors at the same time. I'm writing this chapter during the

COVID-19 pandemic and have seen leaders share their personal stories as a way to connect with their congregants' own experiences. But it's not only global pandemics that we collectively walk through. It could be a church's imminent closure, a nonprofit's layoffs, or the death of a beloved church member. In these times we can minister by sharing our own experience of the valley we are in together with our neighbors.

Normalizing

By sharing our valleys, we open up conversations around taboo and private topics like depression, abuse, infertility, and chronic pain. Speaking up sends a public message that it's okay for us to talk about these topics and makes people aware that these often-unseen experiences exist more widely than they may have believed. For instance, in recent years Christian leaders have, by sharing their stories, helped lessen the stigma around taking mental health medications, going to therapy, and having public conversations about mental health. Pastor Jerry Herships tells me, "I've mentioned my therapist in sermons and in passing, not to make it the point of the sermon, but to normalize it: 'Jerry is just a regular guy like me, and he has a therapist—maybe I should think about it too.'" Our speaking up makes it easier for others to say, "Yes, me too," or to have empathy toward others in circumstances they haven't experienced.

   We can also normalize questions about faith. Many of us have colleagues who think that doubts or probing questions are unworthy of true faith—what pastor Quardricos Driskell describes as "one of the most painful lies" faith leaders have propagated. To push against that notion, Driskell shares from his own faith experiences and points to biblical stories of prophets "who questioned God, but still maintained their faith." He explains, "We often go through things in life that do not make sense and which require us to question God. And God can handle it—we must move past the tyranny of perfection." Instead of erecting a facade, we can share how God is with us, even when we feel alone and when we don't understand where God is leading.

Being a Role Model

Finally, sharing our experiences can provide a role model of faith and vulnerability through difficult seasons. As nonprofit leader Sandhya Jha observes, "I think one of the values I really am trying to model is healthy vulnerability: how do we share our struggles without bleeding onto everybody" when we live in a "culture of needing to withhold our struggles in order to be taken seriously?"

"Part of my job as a pastor," says Jacqueline Lewis, "is to model to my congregants and the world that God can handle us and our stuff." This perspective influences how she shares her life with the congregation she pastors. Telling me about caring for her mother through the illness that preceded her mother's death, she says, "I went home so many weekends in a row—fly out on Thursday, come back on Saturday, and preach in the pulpit. I was exhausted, and I was naked about it. So many people have said to me, 'The way you were public with your grief, the way you were naked with us about your grief, taught us more than anything you could say.' So, amen!"

It may seem as if intentionally being a role model leads to self-glorification. It certainly can, but "as long as we're putting our stories into the service of others, instead of blowing our own horn or being egomaniacs," explains pastor Molly Baskette, "our story can be really instructive and can actually help other people step into their vulnerability and not put us on a pedestal."

We can't always change how others may put us on a pedestal, but by sharing our experiences, we demonstrate something closer to the truth: We fall and get up again. We doubt and yet persist in faith. We question God and yet walk with God.

"I think the healthy expectation for the professional Christian," says pastor Philip DeVaul, "is that we understand what repentance looks like, that we understand what reconciliation looks like, and that we're far enough down the road in our relationship with God that we're not worried that it'll be here today, gone tomorrow." Even as the circumstances of life evolve and our own hearts vacillate, our true relationship with God persists, and we can testify to this reality.

WHEN TO SHARE VALLEYS

As we discern when to share difficult experiences publicly, we should consider two factors.[1] First, whether we have sufficient closure or healing from the valley so that sharing is not part of a therapeutic process. Second, whether we are trying to manipulate care from people who are not appropriate caregivers for us.

To have closure or healing from a challenging experience means that it is in our past or, if it is an ongoing challenge, that we have made peace with it. We may think of the metaphor of scars. We shouldn't share our wounds while we're actively bleeding but should wait to share until we have healed enough to scar.[2] Waiting gives us a chance to get perspective on the valley, even if it is one we will have to live in for our whole lives. This advice holds not only for recent circumstances but for our self-knowledge of failings and how past difficulties have shaped us. "We're all wounded in various ways, and there's nothing the matter with that," explains pastor Paul Rock, referencing a mentor's advice. "The problem is when people don't know they're wounded and end up bleeding on others without even knowing they're doing it."

Waiting to share until we have healed helps ensure we have already found care from appropriate people and not in relationships with lopsided power dynamics such as in a congregational setting or classroom. Our close friends and counselors are the first ones to lend a shoulder, ease our burdens, and help us fumble our way through the fog on the valley's floor.

Waiting to share more widely also helps us avoid manipulation. "You don't want to manipulate people into worrying about you and feeling sorry for you," DeVaul tells me, "but you also don't want to shield people from the truth of your life." Similarly, deVega explains that his congregation knows "that I'm not just unpacking my stuff in front of them" and that he is instead using past experiences to connect with people who are currently struggling.

Sharing our valleys in closer relationships can lead to our healing. In broader relationships, like those we have with congregants, students, or readers, it is about helping others find healing in their own lives. "What I share is an entry point for deeper reflection," says writer Rozella Haydée White, noting that she doesn't share a difficult experience by itself, but connects it with the wider story of her life. She points out that "we all need examples of what it looks like to live an integrated life, because our society does not necessarily provide them." By making those connections visible, she invites people to integrate their own stories.

M.R., a priest, similarly points to the bigger picture, perhaps the biggest goal of sharing valleys: "As ministers we are meant to share the good news—and it is *good* news. In any commentary or sermon, one should walk away with a sense that, yes, this is good news." If we aren't yet at a point where our sharing points to the good news of the Gospel— where we can see the connection of our story to the Gospel—then we are likely not ready to share it in the context of public ministry.

WE DON'T HAVE TO SHARE EVERYTHING

Though sharing valleys can be a powerful form of ministry, we don't have an obligation to turn everything in our lives into a public narrative. Depending on our respective circumstances, we may have more or less capacity to be a role model for how we learn from our failures and flaws; or God may call us to share certain difficult experiences in public ways that most people could not do.

Between the extremes of always and never sharing is a wide range of possibilities informed by our relative comfort with sharing and what we consider private. Imagine privacy at the midpoint, secrecy on one end (with compartmentalizing nearby), and oversharing at the other. What is one person's "too much information" is another person's normal, and what is confidential to one person isn't necessarily personal to another. (Just look at how people introduce their newborns online. Some share a detailed birth story; some post a cute pic with a name and nothing else. Neither approach is necessarily oversharing or withholding.) Knowing that our decisions are context-specific, let's consider compartmentalizing, oversharing, and secrecy to get at a general picture of what healthy privacy and sharing can look like.

Compartmentalizing

Compartmentalizing is one way privacy shows up in our lives. It can simply mean that some aspects of our lives are distinct from others. For instance, I love to cook, but is cooking connected to my public ministry? Unless I'm bringing treats to the choir's Christmas party, not really. My dinner plans are neither private nor a secret. They're just in a different compartment of my life.

In a negative sense, compartmentalizing can also result from having areas of our lives in conflict with each other. "There is compartmentalization that is healthy and lets us function," explains pastor Bruce Reyes-Chow, "and then there's the deceptive compartmentalization that becomes the problem." For instance, when one of pastor Bill Smutz's children was hospitalized with mental-health issues, he shared that difficult season with people close to him but kept it private from the church he pastored, because it wasn't a trusted environment. "I sat in meetings and somebody would ask, 'What joys and concerns do we bring to the table?' I just kept my mouth shut and tried to function as if I wasn't hurting or scared or exhausted."

He explains this was a necessary strategy in the short term but points out the danger of long-term compartmentalizing: it can make us believe that what happens in one part of our lives doesn't affect the rest, because the compartments may alleviate the cognitive dissonance resulting from areas of our lives that can't integrate with others.

Sometimes, as in Smutz's case, we know one part of life is affecting the rest, but we can't share it. That's when compartmentalizing is a helpful short-term strategy.

Oversharing

When we think about being ourselves in ways that harm ministry, oversharing is top of the mind for any of us who have experienced people revealing too much in their professional roles. Who hasn't heard a sermon illustration that left them with wide eyes and the feeling of "Whoa, you need a filter!" This problem is common enough that one of the most consistent threads in my interviews was a practically verbatim exclamation: "The people we serve are not our therapists!"

Researcher Brené Brown describes this kind of oversharing as *floodlighting*—where our neighbors' "emotional (and sometimes physical) response is often to wince, as if we have shone a floodlight in their eyes."[3] Oversharing can pass for authenticity (in the sense of *authenticity as naturalness*), but Brown argues that floodlighting springs not from authenticity but from intentions that "include some combination of soothing one's pain, testing the loyalty and tolerance in a relationship, and/or hot-wiring a new connection ('We've only known each other for a couple of weeks, but I'm going to share this and we'll be BFFs now')."[4] There's also the possible motivation of attention—as the old media saying puts it, "If it bleeds, it leads." If we want eyeballs on us, oversharing reliably provides them.

The impulses to be vulnerable or to get the help we need aren't the problem. The problem is sharing with the wrong people at the wrong time, instead of sharing with close friends and counselors. This kind of oversharing is

directly about confusion in our relationships. To paraphrase Brown, the people we serve are not there to soothe
our pain, to be loyal to us, or to pretend to a relationship that
is deeper than it is.

Secrecy

Secrecy falls at the other end of the spectrum from oversharing. It happens when we hide a private part of our lives
instead of making it known to the appropriate people. In
families and churches, people may control narratives by
using privacy to justify keeping things in the dark, but
secrecy is fundamentally about hiding, not about respecting privacy. With secrecy, the warning that "it's not your
story to share" becomes a tool of manipulation and deception, rather than of respect and caring.

One of the root causes for secrets in churches is a misunderstanding about our relationships with the people we
serve, as when we mistakenly believe they will not be able
to cope with the reality that church people are as flawed
as any others, and that they will be so scandalized by this
reality that they will defect to another congregation or lose
their faith entirely. As a result, we have congregants who
are blindsided when they find out that assistant pastor Bob
abused his spouse or that volunteer Lisa stole the office lap-
top. Instead, we should treat the people we lead as our sib-
lings in the faith—not as tourists passing through—and not
keep secrets out of misguided concerns for congregants.

While we know secrecy perpetuates trauma and
abuse, it can be challenging to identify, because there isn't a
clear line between privacy and secrecy, especially where our
families are concerned. For instance, several interviewees
in addition to Smutz referenced their child's experiences

to illustrate why they couldn't share their own story transparently with their wider community; they couldn't share what they were going through without compromising the child's privacy, because their own emotions and caregiving labor were so entangled with their child's story. This kind of experience is about privacy, not secrecy, because there was nothing fundamentally dishonest about respecting their child's privacy, nor were their actions out of alignment with their values, even though they didn't address the circumstances publicly. In these kinds of situations, wise counselors can help us discern what we can and should disclose and what the parties at the center of the story should determine.

SHARING IN CHURCH SERVICES

Sharing our valleys in church services is a uniquely complicated situation. Even without our intending to, our valleys inform how we lead corporate worship. "Maybe you are going through a rough time in your life," writes pastor and professor Will Willimon, "and your preaching owes more to your reaction to your personal problems than to your exegesis of the Scripture. Perhaps you are preaching for the wrong reasons, improper motivation, the way you were raised as a child, in response to some trauma, or out of your resentment that God has stuck a talented person like you with a congregation of losers like them. Don't worry. A resourceful, redemptive God who turned a cross into a sign of victory can still figure out how to use you."[5]

If we want to intentionally share our valleys in corporate worship settings, we have to begin with why we are personally there; our role and what it entails are what is most important when we're leading corporate worship. For ordained people in particular, Willimon explains, "Your role is not to represent how you're feeling and what you're believing. Your role is to say, 'Here's what the Church teaches, here's what the Bible says, here's what we're trying to believe.'" While not all Christians share Willimon's United Methodist understanding of ordination or shared doctrine, leaders in most congregations are literally *in service* of the whole congregation during a church service. The connection he makes to our shared faith, however loosely or tightly our own church defines it, highlights where the emphasis should be in corporate worship: on Jesus and the Gospel. Meanwhile, our real-time feelings and circumstances as we lead a service are mainly irrelevant to a service as it occurs (something the following chapter considers in more detail).

Sermons in particular are a fraught medium for sharing valleys. As discussed in the context of power in chapter 2, we typically hold the floor while preaching, the setting when we're most likely to overshare in a service. The vast majority of congregants feel a social and religious pressure not to interrupt or leave, which gives us an even greater responsibility to consider our words with care. Oversharing in a sermon doesn't just make us cringe; it's against the sermon's purpose. Sermons come from us, but they are not about us or for us. They are for the whole congregation.

Nonetheless, intentionally sharing valleys can be beneficial, especially when a whole congregation goes through a difficult circumstance together. Pastor Reginald Smith, for instance, notes how important it is for a congregation to be vulnerable "about pain and suffering" that they live through, as well as how "the presence of Jesus shows up in the midst of that" valley. This kind of sharing helps the whole congregation walk with God through the valley, while also showing the broader community "that this is a place where you can bring your pain and brokenness" and find caring people to "walk with you through it."

Despite the caveats, sharing our personal valleys during church services can occasionally aid pastoral ministry. Just as there are benefits of talking about our community's collective valleys, personal sharing illustrates that "God holds everything we bring" to the service, as Reyes-Chow explains. Congregants benefit from hearing leaders point out that church services are not some outside-of-our-lives event where we "are all the sudden perfect or can let everything go.

When we decide if and how to share personal valleys in church services, a critical factor is whether, in our denomination, we are a congregant as well as a leader. Lewis, for instance, can be relatively transparent in her preaching, in part because she is in a tradition (the United Church of Christ) where pastors are members of the congregation, not in a separate category such as a presbytery. She explains, "I can say to the congregation, 'I'm getting ready to preach a sermon, and when I wrote this sermon, I was feeling so fabulous, but at this moment in time, I feel yucky, so pray for me.' My church has space for that for them and for me. . . . In that way, I'm a congregant as well, and I'm not the one outside of the congregation—I'm the one inside the congregation that day, saying, 'Just as I am, without one plea.'"[6]

What is a good fit for Reyes-Chow and Lewis, though, is not necessarily appropriate spiritual leadership in other denominational contexts. None of their scenarios are against their church's doctrine, nor are they attempts to manipulate people in the church. Instead, the sharing that they model draws people into a collective practice of corporate worship.

INTEGRITY IN TRANSITIONS

Keeping valleys private from our wider circle can feel, or even be, disingenuous. So, to help us understand what personal integrity looks like in these seasons, let's consider times of transition. This particular season allows us to see more clearly the bigger picture of situations where not sharing can lead us to feel or be fake.

Some transition periods mark fundamental shifts in our faith, identity, and relationships, which also potentially bring difficult questions of livelihood. A seminarian may realize their beliefs don't align with their denomination's doctrines, but there they are, a semester away from graduating, with a scholarship predicated on becoming a pastor (or maybe they owe tens of thousands of dollars in student loan debt). A teacher, after years in the closet, even to themselves, realizes they are ready to step out of it. But when will they come out, since they will lose their job at their conservative school whenever they make their news public?

Other transitions are more frequent and external, such as when we interview for a new position while leading in our current role as if we will work there indefinitely. Forget the huge questions. Our lives brim with ordinary transitions and common questions about how to discuss them publicly. (Is it wise to voice your own thoughts on Sunday school when your employer/church is going through significant changes to their program? Hmm, I'll get back to you on that!) If we think we will never change, we are falling prey to "the end of history illusion" discussed in chapter 1. Though we often see the change only retroactively, we change throughout our lives, even in old age.

What these transition periods have in common is flux. We may not realize we are entering one until we are in the thick of it, we don't know where the journey will take us, and we may not even know where we want to end up. Cara Meredith, a writer and speaker, recalls being startled when she found herself in the midst of a period she describes as deconstructing her faith. She was in seminary and had worked at a religious nonprofit for years. One day while speaking on stage, she suddenly realized that "everything that was coming out was memorized," so much so, she says, "that there had become a complete lack of connection between my head and my heart." This realization filled her with questions about her faith and identity: "Am I really saying this because I believe this, or am I saying this because it's what I should say? Am I saying this because it's what I'm getting paid to say? Am I saying this because it's the regurgitation of everything I've ever known?"

As with many transition periods, especially ones dealing with faith and identity, finding satisfying answers to these kinds of questions is not quick work. Because of the uncertainty around transitions and the possible ramifications they have for our identity and livelihood, we usually go through them privately, then share the transition once we have a stronger sense of where we have arrived, or at least have paused on the journey. Pragmatically, this can involve considering the financial moves we make. (I think of the pastor I knew who resigned a post around the same time their spouse gained a reliable job.) It also involves having safe places to be completely transparent about our questions and failures (like those close relationships discussed in chapter 1), and possibly seeking out relationships with new mentors to help us grow in the direction we are heading but haven't entirely mapped out. It might mean trying to imagine a future where we fit in our current environment again. Is that possible, or are we so personally changed that our external setting must also change?

Imagine the public side of your life catching up to where your interior journey has gone—or simply your coworkers catching up to the news of your promotion. What is public and what is private eventually align again after the transition period. Your relative silence, though, is not the same as secrecy or lying, nor is it ignoring a fundamental misalignment between self and environment.

Like Meredith, I went through a long season of transition, which influenced me to write this book. As a tween, I began to leave my fundamentalist Baptist upbringing, but because of my limited knowledge of faith, society, culture—really, almost everything—outside of my bubble, and limited opportunities to explore, my exit took about a decade. I have often thought of the lengths I went to pretzel myself into my small world: how I sought the truth while not knowing how to be truly myself, how I sought out counselors even when they rejected my questioning, how I groped in the dark trying to find a window, a door, a light switch—*anything* that would help me find the light. I've wondered whether I had integrity along that journey and whether integrity is a fair value to expect from a sheltered, naive adolescent.

What I do know, though, is something Meredith also found along the way of a complicated, sometimes painful transition: ultimately, truth is what matters. Even when "truth is mystery," she tells me, "instead of doing or saying what you think you're supposed to do or say or believe, be honest and wrestle with the mystery." Sometimes that wrestling is the truest way to be ourselves, no matter how hard it feels at the time.

Amid our valleys, even the dark nights of the soul, we can trust that what is breaking us apart is revealing what is even more true. Barbara Brown Taylor, drawing on John of the Cross, writes that the dark night "is about freeing you from your ideas about God, your fears about God, your attachment to all the benefits you have been promised for believing in God, your devotion to the spiritual practices that are supposed to make you feel closer to God, your dedication to doing and believing all the right things about God, your positive and negative evaluations of yourself as a believer in God, your tactics for manipulating God, and your sure cures for doubting God."[7]

As we walk through the valley—even when we're in the thick of it, unsure how or when we'll ever be able to make it publicly visible—God is with us, comforting us. In that journey, we can grow closer to God and, in so doing, become more truly ourselves.

✳ ✳ ✳

KEY TAKEAWAYS

For the most part, we can't and shouldn't publicly process our valleys, but we may eventually share some valleys to build trust with neighbors, open up conversations around taboo and private topics, and provide a role model of faith and vulnerability through difficult seasons.

As we discern when to share difficult experiences publicly, we should consider whether we have sufficient closure or healing, since this kind of sharing should not be part of a therapeutic process or a manipulative bid for care.

Oversharing, compartmentalizing, and secrecy are often problematic, while privacy is often positive.

Sharing valleys in corporate worship can be pastorally helpful but has potential pitfalls.

Because of the uncertainty around transitions and the possible ramifications they have for our identity and livelihood, we should usually go through them privately, then share the transition once we have a stronger sense of where we have arrived or at least have paused on the journey.

DISCUSSION QUESTIONS

1. What is a valley you have shared publicly?
2. What do you think are positive and negative ways to share valleys?
3. How have you tried to normalize sharing struggles in your circle?
4. Think of times you have seen leaders share a valley. What made those times helpful or made you cringe?
5. How could the compartments in your life become problematic?
6. If you lead corporate worship, what would appropriate sharing in that setting look like for you? What would be inappropriate? As a leader, are you also part of the congregation?
7. If you have gone through a transition in ministry or seen someone else go through one, what kind of integrity did you experience or see?

Chapter 8

FULLY PRESENT IS FULLY OURSELVES

Think back to a time when you had to show up in person to minister, but for some reason you weren't emotionally or physically *there* for it. Maybe you were waiting for a medical diagnosis, but it was Sunday morning and time to sing. Maybe you were officiating at a wedding ceremony during your own caustic divorce proceedings. Maybe it was the emotional whiplash of visiting a dying congregant, then taking the hospital's elevator to a different floor and greeting a healthy newborn and his parents. Maybe you were just tired. You didn't feel like teaching. You didn't want to deal with the volunteers and their needs. All you really wanted was a cup of coffee and a good book.

In this kind of scenario, where our personal emotions differ from those of the people we are ministering to, or where we may not be able to be fully ourselves or what we consider our best selves, *are we being disingenuous?*

If we show up to preach but are feeling apathetic or doubtful, *are we being fake?*

If we are in the depths but in the same moment must lead a congregation in praising God, *are we lying?*

This scenario can happen anytime we engage in *real-time ministry*—anytime we minister in live settings like conversations, classroom teaching, corporate worship, and counseling. Real-time ministry is qualitatively different from modes of ministry that allow time to examine and edit, like writing articles or filming interviews. Real-time ministry has no do-overs, and it gives no significant space for collecting our thoughts or emotionally processing what is happening. We can't, for instance, consider how our histories, identities, or socioeconomic realities impact an in-person conversation as it unfolds, except in the briefest way. We may take in the conversation as it happens, but not be able to digest it—to better understand our emotions, the emotions of others, and other dynamics at play—until later. To be blunt about it, the show must go on. We'll teach the class or lead the song when we must, regardless of how we're feeling about it at the moment.

So where does this reality of ministry meet us? It meets us in the present. And if we are fully present, we are fully ourselves.

By being present with others, we act consistently with the values that brought us to that moment. Showing up to real-time ministry means being present in those times (or at least as present as we can be), while being confident that being ourselves includes our of-the-moment feelings and circumstances, as well as everything else that makes us who we are, like our values, preparation, and vocational calling. We are fully ourselves in the sense that everything in our past, all that brings us to a given moment, is with us in that moment. Our preparation for a sermon is also with us in the preaching of the sermon. The decisions upon decisions that led us to work in a nonprofit are with us in the moments where we struggle to keep our eyes from glazing over in a committee meeting. The value we place on teaching is with us in the classroom.

The real-time is real, and so is everything else about us.

There is no dichotomy here, no need to ignore parts of ourselves. Instead, we can choose to prioritize some elements of ourselves, particularly our curious, mindful attention to the present, knowing that real-time ministry often calls for constraints we can embrace as part of our ministry, and that we can save our introspection for a different time. Our desire to "rejoice with those who rejoice, weep with those who weep" (Rom. 12:15) does not erase our personal emotions and circumstances but orients us toward others' emotions and circumstances, so that we can be in relationship with them where they are.

Even though most ministry roles include real-time aspects, this chapter focuses on pastoral care and leading corporate worship, because these two areas help us examine basic questions about being fully ourselves in the moment. Pastoral care enables us to think about being with another person in their circumstances; leading corporate worship is the situation, of all those we can imagine, where we are supposed to be ourselves in a profoundly spiritual way—to be present as a worshiper who is also leading that worship. These times of pastoral care and leading worship are when we're supposed to be in our most spiritual states, an expectation that makes these times more fraught when we don't feel spiritual. This can lead us to feel as if we're lousy at our jobs or that we're frauds if we are in a season of doubt, don't like the person we are talking with, or simply are tired and still have to sing.

To lay a foundation for these scenarios, let's begin by thinking about thoughtful preparation coupled with careful attention to the present moment. The practices of preparation and mindfulness form the bedrock of being more fully ourselves in real-time ministry.

PREPARATION

As a child in independent Baptist churches, I would hear pastors joke about their colleagues who flew by the seats of their pants: "The Holy Spirit doesn't have to wait until Saturday night. God could have told you what to preach last Monday, if you would have listened!"

In those circles, preachers deeply steeped in biblical knowledge and the craft of preaching could get by with spur-of-the-moment ideas and more than a few well-worn soapboxes. Homiletics professor Eunjoo Mary Kim points out that some people can improvise sermons because of their upbringings—and certainly these preachers were in that group. Some even made their lack of preparation a point of pride for following what they saw as the Holy Spirit's leading. While I don't dispute that the Holy Spirit can lead us at the last minute, I do think the more-prepared preachers were onto something equally true. Since the present is not divorced from the past, our preparation is not outside real-time ministry, but is folded together into it. The preacher who prepared last Monday brings the Holy Spirit's earlier guidance with them into the pulpit on Sunday morning.

Put another way, all of our past is with us in the present, and if we focus only on the real-time moment itself, and not the whole life that includes it, we miss the forest for a single tree, the journey for a single step. "When we live with the Holy Spirit," Kim emphasizes, "our whole process of preparation and preaching is actually the time for the Holy Spirit to work with us." Both the main pillars of our past—education, experiences, and so on—and the more granular aspects of preparation (last Thursday's rehearsal for this Sunday's song set; the time spent months ago selecting a Sunday school curriculum or developing our nonprofit's strategic plan) prepare us to be fully present in the real-time moments of ministry as a both/and experience.

Think again of that sermon preparation. Pastor and diocesan leader Jonathan Arnold offers us the picture of a "lovingly prepared meal," a metaphor that applies to a sermon as much as other aspects of our real-time ministry. Our grandmother's care in prepping the biscuits ahead of time, and the years our uncle has tinkered with the recipe for his secret sauce, are as wholly part of our Sunday meal as our real-time experience of eating it with family. "We prepare as well as we can," Arnold explains, "but then we make sure that once we have the preparation in place, we are then present as ourselves before our God, and in an acknowledgment of the greater purpose of why we are gathered there." As with a family enjoying their Sunday meal together, the congregation can then have "a sense of security that they're in the hands of something that has been lovingly prepared"— regardless of the preacher's own emotions and circumstances in the real-time preaching of their sermon.

MINDFULNESS

Coupled with our preparation is our mindfulness: our purposeful attention to the present. In a therapeutic sense, mindfulness is often about paying attention to our inner experiences of thoughts and physical sensations. But here, I'm thinking particularly about mindfulness to our outer experience of our environment, and more specifically, a mindfulness rooted in caring for the people we encounter in that external environment. "Being present means that you fundamentally really do have to care," notes Arnold. To be present sounds simple, he explains, "but I think what it means is that you engage attentively and seriously with whatever's happening."

Mindfulness in this outward-focused sense necessitates a deep comfort within us about ourselves—a stability that is founded on self-knowledge, a lack of worry about our own selves, and a lack of needing something for ourselves in that moment. With the interior examination set aside for a time, we look outside ourselves and orient our attention toward our neighbors and their needs. We are ourselves always when we are present, when we are mindful, when we are *with* our neighbors, seeing them as they *are*—hungry or thirsty, sick or in prison.

If you are a person who strives to care for your neighbors (presumably a deeply held value for all of us in ministry), then when you give them your full attention, you are acting out of that value. While your own physical experiences and emotions do affect that care, they are secondary to it in the moment. We could think of this as a relationship between a value we hold (that of loving our neighbor) and the action it inspires. Both are part of who we are.

Yet though this focus comes from sincere love, often it doesn't come directly from our gut (our *authenticity as naturalness*), which is why it can feel odd or off. In the moment, we might not *feel* an emotion we'd call caring, but because we do care about our neighbors and about worshiping God, we can be mindful of whatever is happening and give care to anyone we encounter through that mindfulness. Being in the present moment is itself enough, because our outward focus is rooted in caring.

Mindfulness allows us to respond empathetically and realistically. It directs our emotions toward whatever is at hand, while also giving us permission to take time afterward to process an event, make sense of it, and craft a narrative

out of the loose threads. It's the difference between letting a
rough drive to work drag down your whole day and leaving
it in the parking lot, so that you can be present with others
in their circumstances.

Mindfulness makes room for our curiosity and imagination while minimizing boredom. The care that mindfulness requires is a far cry from musical performances I've
seen (and maybe you've seen too) in which the musicians
chugged through the song and dance routine they'd done
hundreds of times before, listlessly sighing their way through
the evening as their *authentic as natural* selves. While their
transparency was in a sense true, it was true neither to the
purpose of the concert (a purpose that presumably was of
value to the musicians) nor to their specific role in the event
(a role that, again, was presumably part of their identity).

Without mindful care, our ministry will be just as
lukewarm as those musicians' performances. We may have
prayed the same Lord's Prayer thousands of times, but
with care we can lead it with our whole hearts once again.
We may have heard the same sad story many times before,
but with care we can attend to the nuances of one person's
individual experience.

PASTORAL CARE

Caring mindfulness grounds our real-time experience of
pastoral care. Real-time pastoral care fixes our attention
on another person, whose circumstances, emotions, and
spiritual state are often different from our own, sometimes
in distressing ways. In these settings, God calls us to be
with that person without judgment, without prematurely
jumping in to fix them or their circumstances, and without

rushing their emotional and spiritual process. Sometimes we minister to and with people we simply don't like, and we must set those feelings to the side. As the saying goes, we don't have to like everyone, but we do have to love them. We "need to be aware of our own attitudes and experiences, and park them at the door," explains Wayne McKenney, an ordained minister who trains military chaplains.

External mindfulness and deliberately minimizing ourselves seem like practices that can lead us to feel disconnected within ourselves. How are we supposed to be fully ourselves if we have to park our attitudes and experiences at the door? Where do our emotions come in? What if the people we are talking with misunderstand who we are?

Pastoral care is a prime site of accepting constraints because of who we are and the values we hold. To "be in the moment with people and be present with them and to witness their emotional state, whatever they're wrestling with, in a pastoral, nonjudgmental, nonanxious kind of way," observes ordained minister and professor Leah D. Schade, requires we put our own feelings aside for the moment, in order to be truly present with another person. Instead of taking the spotlight, we focus on the ones we are caring for— not because our own circumstances aren't important in their own right, but because we are not the priority at the moment.

Pastoral care may also involve a temporary acceptance of others' misperceptions. Pastor Bill Smutz recalls times when *being with* someone has meant making space for something ill-fitting and inaccurate, such as being seen as a "conduit to God." He explains, "When somebody is lying in a hospital bed in their living room dying of cancer, I'm not going to argue with them about what my role is or should be. When I walk in, and I can see the fear in somebody's eyes, my job is to comfort them. And if that means I need to take on this role temporarily, even if it's uncomfortable for me, that's what I need to do."

We must accept the constraints of pastoral care. Otherwise we may gloss over others' difficulties, contextualize others' circumstances (there's always someone worse off, and at least Job wasn't worried about his next meal, right?), or simply get out of there lickety-split. A self-described optimist, writer and speaker Austen Hartke explains, "I have to be very careful when I'm talking to folks who are going through a really difficult thing, so that I don't automatically go into either fix-it mode or Pollyanna mode." If we don't keep this outward focus, we can be tempted to prioritize our feelings and wiggle out of the discomfort that often comes with pastoral care. Writing of integrity in pastoral care, Frank G. Honeycutt warns of the "huge siren call for pastors to fix whatever's wrong and rush past the wreckage to some brighter day in the future. What pastor hasn't breathed a sigh of relief in walking to the hospital parking lot, knowing that the visit is over for now and he is no longer required to stare death down?"[1]

In discussing the role of an ordained person, pastor and professor Will Willimon tells me, "Part of the job is frequently to subordinate, suppress, lay aside personal feelings." He describes situations many of us encounter: we don't feel like showing up at the hospital, we're ministering to someone we don't like, we're in the midst of something personally difficult. And yet, "You have to put that aside, bracket it out, and go ahead and be a pastor, even if it doesn't please you."

We might experience this bracketing as a kind of compartmentalization that is usually healthy but tips toward trouble if, as discussed in the previous chapter, it becomes a long-term strategy or camouflages conflicting aspects of our lives and values. This is one reason for delineating the times of pastoral care, such as through physical rituals. Chaplain Andrew Davis, for instance, uses an intentional deep breath before entering a hospital room to cue him to have "all antennas up" to the "requirements of that moment and the needs of a single person." Marking the threshold of pastoral care helps us integrate this aspect of ministry with the whole fabric of our lives, by consciously bringing our physical selves into the present moment.

In these situations where we are so others-focused, we must recall that our roles and gifts are truly integral to who we are. More than this, our service to others—our rejoicing and weeping that neither denies others' circumstances nor privileges our own experiences—also teaches us about being in our own circumstances and our own selves. Speaker and writer Rozella Haydée White explains that in her experiences, including those as a chaplain, "There is nothing like being fully present in a moment with someone, [recognizing] the reality that you have no control over their situation. In that moment, my role is to be fully present and to be attentive with all of my senses." Being in that mindful, nonreactive space with another person encourages her to practice the same mindfulness with herself: "When I pay attention to that experience, I start to learn more, not only about who I am, but about how I respond to things, and why I respond to things in the way that I do." By being with others in a way that truly prioritizes their experiences, we also learn how to become more truly ourselves.

LEADING CORPORATE WORSHIP

Our experience of leading corporate worship is somewhat different from that of people in the pews because our responsibilities and mindfulness are mostly focused externally. Many of us experience leading—such as through emotive worship elements like preaching, extemporaneous prayer, and solo vocal leadership—as a time when we are "on," that is, in a state of flow. This experience contrasts with most nonleaders' experience of worship, with its potential for introspection and its relative inconspicuousness to the public eye.

When we discover the difference, usually after years of worshiping as a lay congregant, we may feel inauthentic (in the sense of *authenticity as naturalness*) because of how jarring the change is, especially if no one warned us it was coming. Though the new way can involve mundane, even superficial necessities (Molly Baskette isn't the only supervising pastor to remind a seminarian that raised platforms necessitate longer skirts), mostly this change is deep in our hearts. Being fully ourselves in worship isn't the same as before; we have to learn a new way of being ourselves.

Sometimes the change can be so striking that it feels as if leading in worship isn't even *worship*. Smutz, a pastor for more than thirty years, tells me about his experience as a new pastor: "I spent several years trying to find the magic I knew from the late Christmas Eve services of my childhood, even as I was leading the service. And it finally dawned on me one year, 'Oh, this isn't about me. This is about the experience I help other people have.'"

On the other hand, perhaps you, like me, started leading in worship at a young age and later came to realize the reverse—that worship can feel quite different when you are not responsible for leading it. My understanding of worship was a sense of flow, being on, and being visible to others. It wasn't until I was a young adult and began regularly attending services as a nonleader that I realized worship could be a time of introspection and relative anonymity.

(Who knew you could be in a church service and let your attention wander without risking a missed cue?)

What a difference it is to lead worship. It's not that worship leaders do not have profound spiritual experiences or cannot worship during corporate services, but that the experience contrasts with our nonleader experience in the pews. When we're playing the prelude or making sure acolytes are robed, we often aren't able to "enter into a spirit of worship," as some liturgies enjoin the congregation. We are focused on the mechanics of making the service happen— the ordinary troubleshooting and detail work. As a leader of worship, we are focusing outward on others' needs in corporate worship and the goals of the service for the whole congregation.

"It's about some bigger work we're doing together, some bigger energy," says musician Paul Vasile of his outward focus. "It's not just about what I need or want— there are communal needs, values, and desires that are also important." He explains, "If I take the focus off of what I want or need and am willing to temporarily (not always) give myself over to that bigger thing, I fall into a flow that doesn't feel inauthentic, but feels like I'm here for something more than just my own needs and satisfaction."

Theologically, most Christians agree that we can truly worship while leading, whether or not it feels the same as when we aren't leading. Yet I don't want to negate the possibility that, for at least some of us, leading worship can also *feel* like the experience of worship we might have when we aren't leading, especially if we intentionally make room in our preparation and in our theology. Amy Miller describes both to me. In her understanding of corporate worship as an Evangelical pastor, she says, "I believe that every time we meet, God is willing to do some kind of change. It might be a tiny change, but something will get better. And so for me, I'll allow myself to sit in a place of lament. But then I'll also challenge myself to at least take one step out of that." Her preparation for services gives feet to those beliefs by creating practices that allow for spontaneity in services. For instance, she has learned how to sing while kneeling so she can continue leading music while engaging in that spiritual practice. Similarly, in some rehearsals, she has delegated another singer to step in if she is moved to tears.

PERFORMANCE IN CORPORATE WORSHIP

Miller's attention to rehearsal activities that enable her wholehearted worship during a service highlights the second area where we may feel as if we're not being ourselves in leading corporate worship: any element that may require "performance." Depending on your beliefs around leading corporate worship, you may or may not describe your actions as "performance." I use the term here loosely, meaning that you are in front of a group of people, doing public actions to lead them as a whole. In doing these actions, you are being yourself by being in the spiritual role you are called to, one that is the most public way of being fully yourself.

Many of us experience that heightened version of ourselves as being "on" or in a state of flow. Because this state differs from more casual ways of being ourselves, and is so focused on others, we may not recognize ourselves in our actions unless we have become acclimated to the difference. The time passes quickly, over before it's begun. It's when our mistakes are most audible to ourselves and others and, for many of us, also when we're most likely to make adrenaline-fueled errors. Some more seasoned readers may say, "Of course that's still me," but forget how odd, even out of body, the sensation can be when first beginning ministry.

I use the word "performance" here intentionally for another reason—the same reason that some people cringe at it and insist that what we do in leading corporate worship is emphatically not performance. Performance, like the word "acting," carries a connotation of fakery. Of being something not quite yourself (even though you are the one performing). Of intentionally pretending to be someone you're not or deluding yourself in your beliefs about who you are. In worship, the word "performance" carries the possibility that we would put our spiritual leadership on like a mantle and shed it an hour later, our own hearts unchanged.

Performance grates because we know that we *can* be fake. There are leaders who are as fake as the silk flowers around the altar, and preachers with, as pastor Jacqueline Lewis describes it, "a fake preaching voice, a fake talking voice, a fake set of preaching gestures, a fake way to *be* that is your pastor 'you,' your performative 'you.'" With Lewis, we know deep in our hearts that "if you can't be true, you can't teach people to be true. And if you're fake in front of them, then they're going to be fake in front of God."

Fulfilling our leadership role is not fake, regardless of how we feel about it in the real-time moments. We know that leading musical worship in many traditions means modeling enthusiastic, emotive worship in our vocalizing and body movements, but none of us (or at least, no one that I know) always feels on, always feels in the moment as we lead worship, always feels an *authenticity as naturalness* in our actions. We know preaching is something that we must show up as ourselves to do (reading another pastor's sermon out loud isn't "preaching"), but we don't always feel like doing it in the moment. Yet we still must preach. As pastor Paul Rock bluntly put it: "That's not bullshit. That's me doing my job." Paul doing his job is as much Paul as any other time.

What a tension we navigate in our real-time leadership of corporate worship. "The show must go on, and I still have to somehow be uniquely me," says pastor Magrey deVega as he describes his experience preaching. "On the one hand, it is a performance to the degree that the show must go on. Whatever is happening to me, physically or even spiritually, there is a job to do. On the other hand, the actual act of delivering a sermon has to be different from performance. Even when I'm having a rough morning personally, I'm not just delivering lines or reading a manuscript. I'm speaking out of the depths of who I am, even if there are conflicted, inner parts of me in the moment. I have to deliver the sermon in a way that's authentically me, or else it is just watching an actor up there."

Maybe you push back: *Not me! My actions have always come straight from my heart.* I want to ask, have you never spotted your children's shenanigans in the midst of your sermon? Have you never had even the slightest whiff of sickness that distracted you, the tug on your attention warning you that your stomach might not be well? I vividly remember the day I found out I was pregnant with my firstborn, the early morning service with nausea intruding into my thoughts, pulling me out of any kind of flow, and insistently tugging my attention away from my environment and into my own body. An *authenticity as naturalness* read of the situation would say that my spiritual leadership there was lesser or fake. Yes, it was lesser (I accidentally omitted a hymn as I worried whether I would be sick), but I don't think it was fake at all. I was as much myself, persisting through the distraction, as I was on any other Sunday.

The necessity of *keeping on* does not make us fake. Rather, because we have accepted constraints for ourselves by being in ministry roles, we have the imperative to be others-focused and to be with others, with their needs foremost. The feeling of putting on a smile and getting up to preach or sing regardless of how we feel in the moment has nothing to do with *authenticity as naturalness*; as a result it may feel like being fake. But we are being true, not false, when we sincerely fulfill our roles as leaders of corporate worship.

THE HOLY SPIRIT

Throughout this chapter, I have danced around the Holy Spirit, but as I close, it's time to be explicit. The Holy Spirit, in ways we can never fully understand, is always with us, guiding us in our preparation and in our real-time ministry.

The Holy Spirit aims our words toward the hearts of the people we are with. Think of a time when you said (or thought you said) one thing, but someone heard it differently, to their own spiritual benefit. Pastor Reginald Smith describes the times he has preached and had responses about what he supposedly said that left him wondering, "Where in the world did you get that from?" coupled with the fresh realization that "the Lord can take our meager words and allow them to enter into a human heart." Even in times when we haven't felt prepared, we still see the Holy Spirit's work. Describing last-minute requests for pulpit supply, homiletics professor Kenyatta Gilbert says, "I'm often not ready, or at least I don't think I am. But in that moment, I realize that God had been working throughout the whole week to prepare me."

The Holy Spirit is at work in our preparation and our mindfulness. For years, McKenney greeted congregants as they arrived in the church parking lot, often providing pastoral care as people shared raw experiences he couldn't anticipate: "Sometimes they would say, 'Pastor, three days ago, I miscarried.' Or 'My husband filed for divorce.'" Showing up for this ministry right before preaching could have been discombobulating. But, he says, "In a very powerful sense, it was God preparing me and reminding me, *I'm on holy ground.*" That kind of real-time experience points us to the Holy Spirit at work. When we see the fruits of the Holy Spirit, even at our lowest or most distracted points, we remember that the Holy Spirit's work doesn't depend on us.

Writers sometimes joke that only amateurs wait for a mythical muse to appear, whereas professional writers write whether they feel like it or not. Like those amateurs, we can treat the Holy Spirit as a mysterious force that may deign to visit, forgetting that, on the contrary, our callings mean that we show up, and so does the Holy Spirit. We are fully present as ourselves, through the vagaries of what *fully ourselves, fully present* looks and feels like. The Holy Spirit is there too, leading us to holy ground in our preparation and our real-time experiences of ministry.

KEY TAKEAWAYS

By being present with others as the Holy Spirit leads us, we are acting consistently with the values, role, vocational calling, and other preparation that brings us to the present moment.

In real-time ministry, our of-the-moment feelings and gut responses may not match the needs of the circumstance, but we can still minister with a caring mindfulness to our outer environment.

Pastoral care is a prime site of accepting constraints because of who we are and the values we hold, including sometimes temporarily accepting others' misperceptions of us and our roles.

Though leading corporate worship can feel strikingly different from being a layperson in worship, that difference is a sign not of fakeness but of focusing on goals for the whole congregation.

DISCUSSION QUESTIONS

1. When have you felt as if your own emotions didn't match the ministry circumstances you were in?
2. When have you felt fake during real-time ministry? Looking back, were you being fake, or was something else going on?
3. What preparation shapes your real-time ministry?
4. What is your experience of outer-focused mindfulness?
5. What constraints have you accepted in pastoral-care settings?
6. If you have led corporate worship, how have you experienced the difference between being in the pews and having a leadership role? What does "performance" mean to you, and how does that relate to your experiences leading corporate worship?
7. How have you been surprised by the work of the Holy Spirit in your ministry?

CONCLUSION

After matins one summer morning, the incense smoke still lingering in the sanctuary, I stopped to chat with the priest. As a college student finding my way out of fundamentalism, I had been mulling over whether I could, as a "good" Christian, swear. (Don't laugh—I was serious!) Was swearing the "idle word[s]" that Jesus warned against (Matt. 12:36 KJV), I wondered, and pressed him for a cut-and-dried answer.

But Father Ted deflected my questions: "Sarah, you need to love your neighbor."

"I don't see what that has to do with swearing," I responded.

"Sometimes love means you have to get someone's attention."

"So can I swear?"

"Sarah: love your neighbor."

"So I can?"

"Loving your neighbor looks different in different situations. Just love your neighbor."

That conversation profoundly reoriented my perspective on living as a Christian by fixing my eyes on what matters most of all: love. Love is what motivates us to do the difficult work of ministering with our whole hearts by striving to be more fully ourselves. When we are ourselves, we are able to love to our fullest capacities—to love God with our heart, soul, and mind, and to love our neighbors as ourselves (Matt. 22:37, 39).

This love doesn't always look or sound the same. It changes form with different words and new dialects.

Loving a neighbor can be anger at injustice against them.

Loving a neighbor can be relaxing our comfort zone. (Oh, the hugs I get from people who say I need a hug, when truly they are the ones who need it!)

Loving a neighbor can be calling them to account for the sin they commit against another person.

Loving a neighbor can be letting them fail and learn and try again.

Loving a neighbor can be sitting with them in silence, giving them our full attention.

And loving a neighbor can be letting them see Christ in us as we conform more and more into his image.

May we meet the call to be fully ourselves with courage, hope, and, most of all, love.

LIST OF INTERVIEWEES

Jorge Acevedo, Lead Pastor of Grace Church (United Methodist Church; multiple campuses in Southwest Florida) and author of several books, including *Vital: Churches Changing Communities and the World*

Jonathan Arnold, Director of Communities & Partnerships and Rural Life Adviser, Diocese of Canterbury (Anglican) and author of several books, including *Music and Faith: Conversations in a Post-Secular Age*

Molly Baskette, Senior Pastor of First Church Berkeley (United Church of Christ, Berkeley, California) and author of several books, including *Real Good Church: How Our Church Came Back from the Dead, and Yours Can, Too*

Brandy (first name only), professor of theology in discernment for ordination in a mainline denomination

Andrew Davis (pseudonym), Eastern Orthodox priest and chaplain

Philip Hart DeVaul, Rector of The Episcopal Church of the Redeemer (Cincinnati, Ohio)

Magrey deVega, Senior Pastor of Hyde Park United Methodist Church (Tampa, Florida) and author of several books, including *Embracing the Uncertain: A Lenten Study for Unsteady Times*

Quardricos Driskell, Senior Pastor of Beulah Land Baptist Church (Alexandria, Virginia) and federal lobbyist

Brian Erickson, Senior Pastor of Trinity United Methodist Church (Homewood, Alabama) and author of *The Theological Implications of Climate Control: Reflections on the Seasons of Faith*

Phoebe Farag Mikhail, author of *Putting Joy into Practice: Seven Ways to Lift Your Spirit from the Early Church*

Adán Fernández, Director of Music at Holy Family Catholic Community (Glendale, California)

Dan Forrest, composer of many works, including *the breath of life* and *LUX: The Dawn from on High*

Bethany McKinney Fox, Pastor of Beloved Everybody Church (The Presbyterian Church (U.S.A.), Los Angeles, California) and author of *Disability and the Way of Jesus: Holistic Healing in the Gospels and the Church*

Kenyatta R. Gilbert, Professor of Homiletics at Howard University, Baptist minister, and author of several books, including *Exodus Preaching: Crafting Sermons about Justice and Hope*

John Gribowich, Roman Catholic priest

Jude Harmon, Canon for Innovative Ministries, Grace Cathedral (The Episcopal Church, San Francisco, California)

Austen Hartke, speaker and author of *Transforming: The Bible and the Lives of Transgender Christians*

Brian Hehn, Director of The Center for Congregational Song

Jerry Herships, Pastor of Aspen Community Church (United Methodist Church, Aspen, Colorado) and author of several books, including *Rogue Saints: Spirituality for Good Hearted Heathens*

Sandhya Jha, antiracism consultant and speaker, Disciples of Christ minister, and author of several books, including *Transforming Communities: How People Like You Are Healing Their Neighborhoods*

Eunjoo Mary Kim, Professor of Homiletics and Liturgics at Iliff School of Theology, ordained Presbyterian minister, and author of several books, including *Preaching the Presence of God: A Homiletic from the Asian-American Perspective*

Jacqueline J. Lewis, Senior Pastor of Middle Collegiate Church (United Church of Christ and Reformed Church in America, New York) and author of several books, including *Fierce Love: A Bold Path to a Ferocious Courage and Rule-Breaking Kindness That Can Heal the World*

Lakisha R. Lockhart, Assistant Professor of Christian Education at Union Presbyterian Seminary

M. R. (initials only), Roman Catholic priest

Robert McCormick, Organist and Choirmaster of St. Mark's Episcopal Church (Philadelphia, Pennsylvania)

Maria Gwyn McDowell, Rector of St. Philip the Deacon Episcopal Church (Portland, Oregon)

Wayne McKenney, United Church of Christ minister and chaplain

Cara Meredith, speaker and author of *The Color of Life: A Journey toward Love and Racial Justice*

Amy Miller (pseudonym), Evangelical worship pastor

Karen Swallow Prior, Research Professor of English and Christianity and Culture at Southeastern Baptist Theological Seminary, and author of several books, including *On Reading Well: Finding the Good Life through Great Books*

Bruce Reyes-Chow, Pastor of First Presbyterian Church of Palo Alto (The Presbyterian Church (U.S.A.), Palo Alto, California) and author of several books, including *In Defense of Kindness: Why It Matters, How It Changes Our Lives, and How It Can Save the World*

Tanya Riches, Senior Lecturer at Hillsong College (Australia) and author of *Worship and Social Engagement in Urban Aboriginal-Led Australian Pentecostal Congregations*

Brandan Robertson, minister and author of several books, including *Filled to Be Emptied: A Path to Liberation for Privileged People*

Nicole M. Roccas, speaker and author of several books, including *Time and Despondency: Regaining the Present in Faith and Life*

Paul Rock, Senior Pastor of The American Church in Paris (The Presbyterian Church (U.S.A.), France) and co-author of *Jesus, Pope Francis, and a Protestant Walk into a Bar: Lessons for the Christian Church*

Leah D. Schade, Assistant Professor of Preaching and Worship at Lexington Theological Seminary, ordained minister in the Evangelical Lutheran Church in America, and author of several books, including *Preaching in the Purple Zone: Ministry in the Red-Blue Divide*

Braxton Shelley, Associate Professor of Music, of Sacred Music, and of Divinity at the Yale Institute of Sacred Music, Yale Divinity School, and Yale University's Department of Music, ordained minister, and author of *Healing for the Soul: Richard Smallwood, the Vamp, and the Gospel Imagination*

Anita Smallin, Director of Youth and Family Ministry at Trinity Lutheran Church (Evangelical Lutheran Church in America, Bethesda, Maryland)

Reginald Smith, ordained minister and Director for Offices of Race Relations and Social Justice at the Christian Reformed Church

Kim Smolik, Partner of Leadership Roundtable

William M. Smutz, Interim Senior Pastor at First Presbyterian Church of Kirkwood (The Presbyterian Church (U.S.A.), Kirkwood, Missouri)

Lydia Sohn, writer and United Methodist minister

Casey Stanton, Roman Catholic educator and lay leader

Nikki Toyama-Szeto, Executive Director of Christians for Social Action

Paul Vasile, Director of Music at Eden Theological Seminary and Executive Director of Music that Makes Community

Rozella Haydée White, consultant and author of *Love Big: The Power of Revolutionary Relationships to Heal the World*

Will Willimon, Professor of the Practice of Christian Ministry at Duke Divinity School, bishop in the United Methodist Church (2004-2012), and author of many books, including *Preachers Dare: Speaking for God*

Laura Wilson (pseudonym), Baptist minister to children

Two additional unnamed interviewees serving as an Evangelical worship pastor and a pastor of a mainline congregation

ACKNOWLEDGMENTS

To all the ministry leaders I interviewed while writing this book, I am grateful for the grace you showed me, the wisdom you shared, and the way you opened your hearts. I could not have written this book without you.

Diana, Bill, Cole, Ana, Lee (a.k.a. Mom!), and Rick: Thank you for listening to me talk about authenticity and all things writing-related for many, many conversations—and for always building me up.

Father Ted and Father Steven, when I wrote about pastoral care and ministry throughout this book, I had a clear picture of what it can be at its best because of you two.

Margaret Watson and Gerald N. Carper, thank you for letting God use you to guide my path to ministry. I think you saw my call many years before I could recognize it for myself.

Thank you to my colleagues and the congregation at the First Congregational Church of St. Louis for supporting my writing of this book.

Thank you to the wonderful people who helped me learn how to write (and think) in book form, particularly Philip Rupprecht, Jacqueline Waeber, Louise Meintjes, and Jeremy Begbie.

Thanks to the team at Westminster John Knox for bringing this book into the world, especially Jessica Miller Kelley (how much better this book is because of your editing!), Julie Tonini, Hermann Weinlich, and Heather Hart.

Thank you to David Greenhaw and Kirsten Santos Rutschman for your close and generous reading. I am so blessed that you took the time, the energy, the everything to read my wonky drafts. David, I found myself in my book because of your insights, and you dialed my blur into focus. Kirsten, you identified many areas to improve and helped me better include readers.

Brandon and Crawford, thank you for listening to me and supporting me. In treating my work with love and respect, you have made me feel so valued. Crawford, you know my writing voice better than I myself know it. How grateful I am to be seen.

I thank God for you all!

NOTES

Introduction

1. C. S. Lewis, *The Screwtape Letters, with Screwtape Proposes a Toast* (1942; repr., New York: HarperSanFrancisco, 2001), 65: "when they are wholly His they will be more themselves than ever."
2. Donna Haraway originated the term in her essay "Situated Knowledges: The Science Question in Feminism and the Privilege of Partial Perspective," *Feminist Studies* 14:3 (Autumn 1988): 575-99.
3. For you Enneagram buffs, yes, I know: classic 3w4.

Chapter 1: The Foundation for Being Fully Ourselves

1. Cynthia G. Linder, *Varieties of Gifts: Multiplicity and the Well-Lived Pastoral Life*, foreword by Martin E. Marty (Lanham, MD: Rowman & Littlefield, 2016), 23.
2. Linder, *Varieties of Gifts*, 23.
3. Jordi Quoidbach, Daniel T. Gilbert, and Timothy D. Wilson, "The End of History Illusion," *Science* 339 (January 2013): 96-98.
4. Quoidbach et al., "The End of History," 96.

5. Priya Parker, *The Art of Gathering: How We Meet and Why It Matters* (New York: Riverhead Books, 2018), 216.

6. Nicole M. Roccas, "Learning to Be Oneself: A Spiritual Discipline?" Ancient Faith Ministries, November 28, 2018; https://blogs.ancientfaith.com/timeeternal/learning-to-be-oneself/.

Chapter 2: Power, Pedestals, and Other Complications of Professional Ministry

1. Harry G. Frankfurt, *On Bullshit* (Princeton: Princeton University Press, 2005), 63.

2. Frankfurt, *On Bullshit*, 64.

3. Gretchen Rubin, *The Four Tendencies: The Indispensable Personality Profiles That Reveal How to Make Your Life Better (and Other People's Lives Better, Too)* (New York: Harmony Books, 2017).

Chapter 3: Authenticity, Sincerity, and Other Ways to Imagine How to Be Ourselves

1. George Lakoff and Mark Johnson, *Metaphors We Live By* (Chicago: University of Chicago Press, 1980).

2. These insights on "real" and "fake" authenticity are from Andrew Potter, *The Authenticity Hoax: How We Get Lost Finding Ourselves* (New York: Harper, 2010), 14, 125–35.

3. Lionel Trilling, *Sincerity and Authenticity* (Cambridge, MA: Harvard University Press, 1972), 58.

4. Trilling, *Sincerity*, 58.

5. William Shakespeare, *As You Like It*, 2.7.139–144 (Boston: D. C. Heath, 1916).

6. "Personally expressive," "star persona," and "song persona" are from Simon Frith, *Performing Rites: On the Value*

of Popular Music (Cambridge, MA: Harvard University Press, 1996), 186, 212.

7. Thanks to a friend for pointing out the pun.

8. Brené Brown, *Daring Greatly: How the Courage to Be Vulnerable Transforms the Way We Live, Love, Parent, and Lead* (New York: Gotham Books, 2012), 34.

9. See for example, Brown, *Daring Greatly*, 45; and *Dare to Lead: Brave Work. Tough Conversations. Whole Hearts.* (New York: Random House, 2018), 34–35.

Chapter 4: Communicating with Neighbors We Know—And Those We Don't

1. My thinking on mediation, and how we often forget about it, has its genesis in Jonathan Sterne's writing on recording as a "vanishing mediator" between live music and listener, in *The Audible Past: Cultural Origins of Sound Reproduction* (Durham, NC: Duke University Press, 2003), 218; after Fredric Jameson, *Ideologies of Theory*, vol. 2. (Minneapolis: University of Minnesota Press, 1988), 3–34; and Slavoj Žižek, *For They Know Not What They Do: Enjoyment as Political Factor* (New York: Verso, 1991), 179–88.

Chapter 5: Skewed Reality or a Slice of Life?

1. Harry G. Frankfurt, *On Bullshit* (Princeton: Princeton University Press, 2005), 60–61.

2. Frankfurt, *On Bullshit*, 55.

3. Frankfurt, *On Bullshit*, 60.

4. Craig C. Hill, *Servant of All: Status, Ambition, and the Way of Jesus*, foreword by William H. Willimon (Grand Rapids: Eerdmans, 2016), 94.

5. Hill, *Servant of All*, 134.

6. Hill, *Servant of All*, 150.

Chapter 6: For the Sake of Our Neighbors

1. Leah D. Schade, *Preaching in the Purple Zone: Ministry in the Red-Blue Divide* (Lanham, MD: Rowman & Littlefield, 2019).

2. "God's work. Our hands." is the tagline of the Evangelical Lutheran Church in America.

3. Jean Kidula, interview with Sarah Bereza, "Music and the Church with Sarah Bereza," podcast audio, November 11, 2019; https://sarah-bereza.com/44.

Chapter 7: Sharing Our Valleys with Others (Or Not)

1. These two factors came up repeatedly in my interviews, and researcher Brené Brown identified similar factors in her own discerning process, as well as the process used by many other people with public-facing work, in her *Daring Greatly: How the Courage to Be Vulnerable Transforms the Way We Live, Love, Parent, and Lead* (New York: Gotham Books, 2012), 161–62.

2. Several interviewees quoted Nadia Bolz-Weber specifically regarding wounds and scars, but the metaphor is older.

3. Brown, *Daring Greatly*, 160.

4. Brown, *Daring Greatly*, 159.

5. Will Willimon, *Preachers Dare: Speaking for God* (Nashville: Abingdon, 2020), 107.

6. Lewis quotes from the hymn "Just as I am, without one plea" by Charlotte Elliot, *The Hymnal 1982* (New York: Church Publishing, 1985), 693.

7. Barbara Brown Taylor, *Learning to Walk in the Dark* (New York: HarperOne, 2014), 145.

Chapter 8: Fully Present Is Fully Ourselves

1. Frank G. Honeycutt, *The Truth Shall Make You Odd: Speaking with Pastoral Integrity in Awkward Situations* (Grand Rapids: Brazos Press, 2011), 97.

CPSIA information can be obtained
at www.ICGtesting.com
Printed in the USA
LVHW031151100322
712579LV00003B/6

9 780664 266714